Everyday Life in the New Nation 1787–1860

About the Book

In the years between the founding of the United States and the Civil War there was a transformation from an agricultural to an industrial nation. It was an era of great excitement and change. In this book authors Louis B. Wright and Elaine W. Fowler discuss these events dramatically. Here are described hardships and pleasures, the diversions of politics, the adventures of travel, the lure of life at sea. The entire social life of an expanding nation is discussed in entertaining detail.

Everyday Life
in the New Nation
1787–1860

BY LOUIS B. WRIGHT
AND ELAINE W. FOWLER

G. P. PUTNAM'S SONS, NEW YORK

917.3
W

Contents

LIFE IN  AMERICA

Edited by Louis B. Wright

Everyday Life In Colonial America
by Louis B. Wright

Everyday Life in Twentieth Century America
by John W. Dodds

Everyday Life in the Age of Enterprise
by Robert H. Walker

Everyday Life on the American Frontier
by Louis B. Wright

Everyday Life in the New Nation
by Louis B. Wright and Elaine Fowler

Preface

In the space permitted in this brief book, the authors have tried to convey to the reader an idea of the excitement and change taking place in America between the years 1787 and 1860, between the Constitutional Convention and the eve of the Civil War. We have sought to do this without duplicating material in another volume in this series, *Everyday Life on the American Frontier*, which will serve as a complement to the present volume. Obviously in the compass of a short book we could not tell in detail the history of the country in these momentous years, but we have attempted at least to suggest a few of the important events.

The years before the Civil War saw the United States extend its territories to the Pacific Ocean and begin the transformation from an agricultural to an industrial society. Before 1860 the great bulk of the population was still rural, and not until 1920 did the census show a preponderance of the population living in cities. In consequence, living conditions in much of the United States had changed little since colonial days. The frontier was still primitive with a great premium placed on the ingenuity and versatility of the individual settler.

The revolution in transportation, which has reached a culmination in our time in jet aircraft exceeding the speed of sound, began in this period. Robert Fulton's steamboat, the *Clermont*, on the Hudson River in 1807 was the forerunner of faster traffic on rivers and the oceans. The little locomotive the Best Friend of Charleston, dragging its cars along the Charleston and Hamburg line in 1830, was the herald of land transportation that would knit the country into a network of railways that only now, in the opinion of some, are becoming obsolete.

Each chapter in this volume would warrant a book in itself, and the authors can only hope that the reader will want to pursue the various topics at greater length. We have appended a short list of books that will provide more detailed information.

L. B. W.
E. W. F.

Everyday Life
in the New Nation
1787–1860

Chapter 1

The Creation of a
New Nation

No radio or television informed Americans on July 4, 1776, that the Continental Congress had just agreed to accept the Declaration of Independence drawn up by its distinguished committee of five, whose chief draftsman was Thomas Jefferson. News traveled more slowly in those days. Four days later, at noon on July 8, a crowd in front of the State House in Philadelphia heard this historic document read to them, and on July 10 the *Pennsylvania Journal* published it. Other little newspapers throughout the length and breadth of the land copied the *Journal*'s version, and the news gradually reached the far corners of what had been Great Britain's thirteen colonies. No longer did George III reign from Maine to Georgia. Thirteen colonies had become thirteen sovereign states, and a new nation had come into being. But as yet it was a nation only in theory, for nations, like people, are usually born in travail and suffering.

At the time the Declaration of Independence was submitted to the Congress for approval, Richard Henry Lee made a proposal for a permanent union of the former colonies, and a committee was appointed to draw up a plan of union. In November, 1777, Articles of Confederation were approved by the Congress, but it took until March, 1781, for the states to ratify the Articles.

In the meantime the Congress, which had no power of taxation, conscription, or coercion of the states, had to try to coordinate the activity of the armies fighting the British and to persuade the individual states to support the war with supplies and levies of men. The ultimate success of the Americans was a miracle partly accounted for by the courage, persistence, and wisdom of a few leaders, chief of whom was George Washington.

The refusal of the states to surrender any jot of their sovereignty to a central government virtually annulled the definition of the thirteen states as a workable nation. Each state was in effect an independent country with the power to tax, appoint its own officials, levy duties, and decide how and whether it would cooperate with the others. The Articles of Confederation made only a slight improvement in this situation. They established a Congress very much like the old Continental Congress, with delegates appointed by the state legislatures. The Congress had no power within the states but was to act for the states in foreign affairs, make treaties, borrow money and issue currency, serve as an admiralty board and have control over American affairs at sea, determine uniform weights and measures, maintain a postal service, have general oversight of Indian affairs, and serve as a court in disputes between the states.

Obviously so loose an organization could not evolve into a nation efficiently governed, but it required more than a decade for Americans to overcome their fear of substituting another tyranny for the rule of George III that they had so recently thrown off.

In the meantime, conditions throughout the country were going from bad to worse. Everywhere men complained of hard times. The money issued by the Continental Congress depreciated until it became a byword, and the phrase "not worth a Continental" meant utter worthlessness. Debtors could not pay their taxes and interest on loans. When the courts ordered farms and homes sold for debt, public outrage grew into violence. In western Massachusetts a veteran of the War of Independence, Daniel Shays, organized a ragged army which he led against Springfield with the avowed purpose of overturning a government that supported tyrannical courts that ordered poor men's property sold to satisfy mortgages.

Although "Shays' Rebellion" was promptly suppressed, it sent a shiver of fear throughout the colonies. In other areas there were threats of violence. Business was poor everywhere. The War of Independence had disrupted commercial relations with Great Britain and ruined many merchants. The end of the war and the treaty with Great Britain in 1783 had not meant an immediate restoration of cordial business relations. Quarrels over debts owed to British subjects persisted for years. During the war American industries had developed to supply the market with goods formerly obtained from Great Britain, and American weavers, ironmongers, pewterers, copper- and silversmiths, cabinetmakers, and many other craftsmen had laid the foundations of businesses that they hoped would flourish with independence. To their consternation, after the war Great Britain dumped finished goods on the market at prices cheaper than Americans could produce them, and American laborers found themselves out of work. As in every war, a few profiteers had got rich and flaunted their new wealth. Men with money, some of them notorious war profiteers, at vastly depreciated prices had bought up bonds issued during the war by the Continental Congress and the states. They were gambling on the bonds' ultimate redemption at face value. The movement to guarantee the payment of these bonds became a matter of acrimonious controversy.

In every state factions developed, and radical politicians whipped up prejudice with talk about the oppression of the

13

rich. The states themselves were jealous of each other and could not agree about commercial rights. For example, interstate quarrels included a tariff war between New York and New Jersey and squabbles elsewhere over the control of waterways traversing more than one state. Western lands were also a fruitful source of envy and complaint that would persist for generations to come. For a long time Atlantic coast colonies, whose charters granted them land across the continent to the "Great South Sea" (the Pacific Ocean), had quarreled over their conflicting claims to land in the West. By 1786, however, these states had ceded their claims to lands north of the Ohio to the Congress, and the Congress issued the Ordinance of 1787 establishing the Territory Northwest of the Ohio. One notable provision of the Northwest Ordinance was the exclusion of slavery in this territory. But the Ordinance of 1787 did not end quarrels over land rights in the West.

Conditions had reached such a threatening state by the winter of 1786–87 that moderates of various factions and conservatives everywhere realized that something must be done. They feared that radicals, who had been denouncing the rich (what today we would call the Establishment) and in fact everyone in power, were ready to overturn the state governments and substitute chaos. Against this background, the states appointed delegates to a convention which met in Philadelphia on May 25, 1787, to consider amending the Articles of Confederation to create a stronger central government. This convention produced the Constitution under which we still live, a document remarkable for its farsighted wisdom and its capacity to accommodate diverse factions which had nearly wrecked the infant nation in its first decade.

The Constitution of 1787 was not adopted without months of debate in which conservatives and radicals fought over every issue. By compromise, bargain, and in some instances the use of steamroller tactics, the convention agreed on a platform of government that owed much of its

14

theory to the English philosopher John Locke, its counterbalancing legislative, executive, and judicial branches to the French political thinker Montesquieu, and its good sense to what John Dickinson called the guide of experience. "Reason may mislead us," he warned. "Experience must be our only guide."

Some historians have argued that the men who put through the Constitution of 1787 were holders of property intent upon preserving rights to property. That the influential majority who drafted the Constitution were conservatives who feared radicals is true, but they were also patriotic men of wisdom, intent upon creating an instrument of government that would guarantee a stable society which they believed would result in the greatest good to the greatest number.

Having drafted this document, the convention adjourned on September 17, 1787, and sent it out to the states for ratification. Debate over the Constitution in the state legislatures was frequently violent. In Pennsylvania, for example, radical members of the legislative assembly were so opposed to ratification that they planned to stay away from sessions of the assembly and thus prevent a quorum that could vote on it. But a pro-Constitution mob in Philadelphia hunted out the radical members, dragged them to the sessions, and held them in their chairs until a vote was taken that ratified the Constitution. Delaware was the first state to ratify and was followed by Pennsylvania, New Jersey, Georgia, and Connecticut. After a great debate Massachusetts ratified, and it was followed by Maryland, South Carolina, and New Hampshire. Virginia and New York did not get around to ratifying until the summer of 1788; North Carolina waited until November, 1789, and Rhode Island, most radical of the states, did not ratify until 1790. Thus were the states at last welded into a union that its creators hoped would be perpetual. Ultimately it took a civil war to test its permanence and prove it indissoluble.

The Constitution had provided for a Congress with a

15

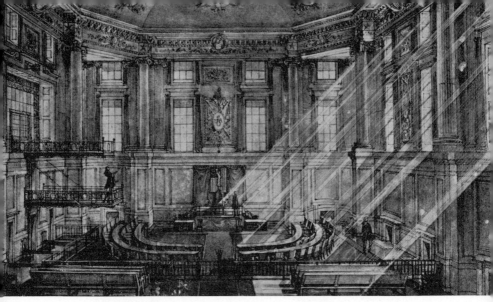

The Chamber of the House of Representatives in Federal Hall, New York. Then as now, the Speaker (Frederick A. Muhlenberg) frequently addressed empty seats. *Anonymous engraving. Courtesy, Library of Congress.*

Senate and a House of Representatives and with a President elected by an electoral college chosen by the states, so fearful were the conservatives of election by the populace, who might choose a wild man for this most important office. The new Constitution gave more power to the central government over the states than King George and the English Parliament had ever exercised over the colonies. For that reason many citizens in all the states opposed ratification of the Constitution, and the question of states' rights, which continues to be a controversial problem to the present day, was a matter of ardent debate.

But after ratification by all the states except North Carolina and Rhode Island, plans went ahead for the organization of the new government. The last Congress under the Confederation in August, 1788, ordered elections to be held for a President, and George Washington was elected. John Adams of Massachusetts was chosen Vice President, an office which he described as "the most insignificant . . . that ever invention of man contrived or his imagination conceived." The date for the new government to take office

16

had been set for March 4, 1789, but not until the last day of April was the organization sufficiently complete for the President to be inaugurated. The capital was established temporarily in New York City. There on April 30 George Washington, standing on the balcony of Federal Hall on Wall Street, took the oath of office as first President of a country with a frame of government that promised permanence.

The choice of Washington as President was fortunate, for no man had greater prestige in the nation, and if anybody could unite the quarrelsome elements in society, he could. But he realized the magnitude of his task. As he left his comfortable home at Mount Vernon to go to New York, he wrote to a friend that he felt like a "culprit, who is going to the place of his execution, so unwilling am I, in the evening of a life nearly consumed in public cares, to quit a peaceful abode for an ocean of difficulties, without that competency of political skill, abilities, and inclination which are necessary to manage the helm."

As Washington realized, the difficulties facing him were great, for the nation had no trained body of civil servants, no money in the treasury and no tax system as yet to raise money, and not even an organized judicial system for enforcing such laws as might be passed. Furthermore, the great European powers with an interest in America—Eng-

The inauguration of Washington as first President of the United States took place on April 30, 1789, at Federal Hall in New York. This early seat of the Congress stood at the corner of Wall and Broad streets, lower, Manhattan. Engraving by A. Doolittle after Peter Lacour. Courtesy, Library of Congress.

land, France, and Spain—were waiting like birds of prey to pounce on the little nation and use it for their own gain. It would take skill, wisdom, and luck to steer the ship of state into a safe port, as Washington knew, and he set about choosing the best officers he could find to help him.

For Secretary of State Washington appointed Thomas Jefferson, who was completing a tour of duty as minister to France; for Secretary of the Treasury, Alexander Hamilton, a conservative New Yorker. These two important members of the Cabinet were exact opposites in their political and social views. Jefferson, principal author of the Declaration of Independence with its ringing phrase about "life, liberty, and the pursuit of happiness," had infinite faith in the common people. He hoped that America would develop into a prosperous agricultural country, a land of virtuous farmers much like republican Rome as he imagined it. In the growth of towns and the increase of industry he saw infinite dangers. To Jefferson the best government was one that required the least interference of the governing authority. Hamilton, on the contrary, distrusted the common people and thought that too much power in the hands of the populace would lead to what he called "mobocracy" and anarchy. He believed that a strong central government was necessary to maintain law and order. Lacking Jefferson's faith in a nation of virtuous citizens living on the land, Hamilton wanted to encourage industry and commerce to ensure the country's economic strength. The divergent beliefs of these two powerful leaders were indicative of the ideas that would in time dominate the two political parties, liberal and conversative, that would arise. Jefferson became the leader of what was then called the Republican (now Democratic) Party; Hamilton became one of the chief spokesmen for the Federalist Party, the ancestor of the modern Republican Party.

Washington at first hoped that the Presidency could stand above parties, but that ideal proved a delusion. For the executive to get his policies accepted he had to have the support of a party behind him and be an influential member of that party. Washington soon threw in his lot with the Federalists, with whom he was in sympathy, for he was too much of a political realist to share Jefferson's faith in the wisdom of the generality of the people.

During Washington's first administration Hamilton and Jefferson were often at variance in their views, but they managed surprisingly to compromise on a number of important matters and reach a working agreement. For example, Hamilton's financial policy was designed to stabilize and insure the credit of the nation. In order to do this, he insisted upon guaranteeing the payment at par of foreign and domestic loans made by the Continental Congress and the bonds issued by the state governments during the War of Independence. Jefferson agreed to the assumption of the foreign and domestic debts but was dubious about guaranteeing all the state bonds which had been bought up by speculators at low prices. He felt that honest citizens would be burdened with taxes to enrich shrewd operators who had gobbled up depreciated bonds acquired for a song. Hamilton argued that demonstrable proof of the financial integrity of the country required full payment of all these obligations even if some rascals got rich as a result. Jefferson agreed to go along with this policy, but he saw an opportunity to drive a shrewd bargain. If Hamilton would persuade the Northern states to vote to move the national capital to a site on the Potomac River, Jefferson would persuade Virginia Congressmen to vote for the assumption of the state debts. So that is how the Federal City of Washington came to nestle upon a marsh on the banks of the Potomac. The temporary capital was moved from New York to Philadelphia for ten years while the Federal City was being laid out and enough houses were built to accommodate the government and its officials.

At the end of his first term in 1792 Washington was eager to retire to his farm at Mount Vernon, but both Jefferson and Hamilton persuaded him to accept a second term, to which he was elected without opposition. Some conservatives even wanted to make Washington king, but the Virginia planter gave no encouragement to such nonsense as he deemed it. Jefferson distrusted Hamilton's "monarchical" views but was certain that Washington was too true a patriot to be persuaded to accept even a life post as head of state. So all factions united to induce the President to serve one more term. But though Washington was unopposed in 1792, the election showed the growing strength of discontented voters calling themselves Republicans (Democrats today). As leader of this party, by the end of the year 1793 Jefferson felt that he could no longer remain in a bipartisan Cabinet with propriety, particularly since members of his party were beginning to make vicious attacks on the President himself. Consequently, on December 30, 1793, Jefferson resigned as Secretary of State with the intention of retiring to his farm at Monticello. Through a long life of varied political activities Jefferson was always yearning for retirement to Monticello. Both Washington and Jefferson found greater satisfactions in their plantations than in their political achievements, but each relinquished retired ease to serve his country in accordance with his conscience and his individual political beliefs.

By the beginning of Washington's second term in office the national government was fairly well organized. Some of the most difficult problems had been faced and solutions found or proposed. Politics had begun to polarize into a two-party system which would endure to the present time. And European nations had ceased to believe that the United States would dissolve into chaos that would give them a chance to pick up choice pieces. The nation was established, and though then, as always, it had many vexing problems to deal with, its future seemed assured.

Chapter 2

Politics—Diversion for Everybody

From the early days of the Republic, Americans have shown a vigorous concern about the state of the nation and have been highly vocal in expressing their opinions. As conservative and liberal parties aligned themselves into Federalists and Republicans (Democrats) in Washington's second administration, hardly a blacksmith, tinker, carpenter, merchant, or farmer from Maine to Georgia failed to express his views at gatherings around the forge, in taverns, at social events, or formal meetings. Not everyone could vote, for the doctrine of one man, one vote was still long years in the future, but everybody had an opinion which he did not hesitate to express, often in violent complaint, for Americans have rarely been content with their governments of whatever party. Problems concerning debt, taxation, trade, speculation in land, Indian threats on the frontier, foreign threats from abroad, piracy on the high seas, and scores of other matters engaged the attention of American citizens and troubled their political representatives.

Although Americans thought of themselves as a long way from Europe, not even in this early time could they remain isolated from events overseas. Even if it took weeks or months for ships to bring messages, men, and cargoes across the Atlantic, the European wars, trade, and politics eventually affected every man, woman, and child in the United States. So it was that the outbreak of the French Revolution in 1789 had profound repercussions in this country.

France had come to the aid of the colonies when they were fighting for independence from Great Britain. France had provided loans of money, munitions and supplies, men, and ships that had helped win the war. On February 6, 1778, Benjamin Franklin, as a commissioner authorized by the Continental Congress, had signed a treaty of alliance with France, which remained in effect. Throughout the country Americans felt a sense of gratitude to the country that had supported them in a time of dire need and had ensured their independence.

Although the American Revolution had not been a revolution that transformed the social system as did the Russian Revolution of 1917, it was a dramatic and successful overthrow of royal authority, of the "tyranny of kings," and was so interpreted in Europe. The example of the American colonies' successful struggle for independence and liberty encouraged discontented Europeans everywhere who dreamed of emulating the Americans.

It would be an oversimplification to say that France caught the contagion of revolution from America as it might catch a disease. For more than a generation Frenchmen had been discussing political theories more revolutionary than those of the American colonists, and misgovernment, hard times, and poverty in France in the later years of the eighteenth century were sufficient reasons for unrest and rebellion. But French patriots like Lafayette, who had fought on the American side, undoubtedly carried back American ideas of reform that they tried to implement. And Frenchmen made heroes out of Americans who represented the liberty-loving country. Benjamin Franklin, for example,

The Marquis de Lafayette bids farewell to General Washington and his family at Mount Vernon, where he had been a frequent visitor. *Lithograph published by E. Farrell, 1784. Courtesy, Library of Congress.*

who served as an effective agent for the colonies during the War for Independence, was lionized by all France. Wearing his fur cap to symbolize to Frenchmen the quality of the simple and heroic frontiersman, Franklin aroused their imaginations and won friends by the thousands for his country. When Thomas Jefferson succeeded him as minister in France, as the French Revolution was gathering force, French reformers consulted him about proposed changes in their government. Jefferson, it should be remembered, urged his eager French friends to be cautious. At this time he did not believe that France ought to throw off the rule of Louis XVI, for he doubted the capacity of the French populace for self-government. The kind of government suitable for America might not be suitable for France. Though Jefferson later defended the actions of French revolutionaries and was accused by his enemies at home of being a Jacobin (which was equivalent to calling him a Communist today), he advised reformers who sought his advice to strive for a constitutional monarchy like England's.

But conditions in France were too volatile for a peaceful reform of the government, and the more militant elements

23

gained ascendency. The king was dethroned and guillotined on January 21, 1793. In the meantime, Americans had followed the news from France with avid interest. When the story of the fall of the Bastille on July 14, 1789, reached America, it had set off celebrations throughout the country. For the next four years the liberals in America had been ardent partisans of the French revolutionaries. The violence of the French populace, however, aroused the fears of American conservatives, who saw in their "barbarism" the shape of things that might come to America. Soon the attitude of Americans toward the French became a political touchstone: enthusiasm for the French indicated a Republican (Democrat); hostility was certain to label a man a Federalist.

This polarization did not develop immediately, for in the beginning, enthusiasm for the French effort to throw off tyranny was widespread throughout the country. When Lafayette sent President Washington the key to the fallen Bastille, Washington wrote him a cordial letter of thanks for this symbol of the victory over despotism. A few years later, however, Washington would have been condemned by his fellow Federalists for such a letter.

Enthusiasm for the French Revolution reached a fever pitch in America late in 1792 and early in 1793. To thousands of Americans the establishment of a republic after the overthrow of the monarchy meant another government, they thought, like their own, a great and powerful republic which would be a bulwark for the United States.

Celebrations glorifying the French Republic took place throughout the country, and no man can estimate the quantity of rum punch consumed in drinking toasts to France, liberty, equality, and the inalienable rights of man.

One of the first gala celebrations took place in Baltimore on December 20, 1792. A local newspaper reported that "a numerous and respectable company of gentlemen, Friends of the Rights of Man," met at the Fountain Inn "for the purpose of celebrating the late triumph of liberty over despotism in France." After a bountiful dinner they drank

24

"fifteen republican toasts."[1] and at length staggered home full of liquor and warm with zeal for liberty and fraternity.

The celebration in Baltimore was only the beginning of a rash of dinners, parades, pageants, barbecues, and oratorical orgies glorifying the French republicans. Two days after Christmas in 1792 New York set up a liberty pole topped by a red liberty cap. At the society hall of St. Tammany, called the Wigwam, the celebrants held a convivial banquet where liquor and eloquence flowed in torrents. Some republicans were moved to song; one of these lyrical outbursts concluded:

> May heaven continue still to bless
> The arms of freedom with success,
> Till tyrants are no more;
> And still as Gallia's sons shall fly
> From victory to victory,
> We'll, shouting, cry "Encore!"

The climax of extravagant celebration, however, took place in Boston on January 24, 1793. This was three days after the beheading of Louis XVI, but of course that news had not yet reached this side of the Atlantic. Boston outdid itself in what was described in the newspapers as a great "Civic Feast," a compliment to French citizens who had "rendered essential services to the establishment of Liberty and Independence in America in the former conflict with Great Britain." The French Republic, which had been attacked by monarchist powers of reaction, had driven back the Prussians. When this news reached Boston, it set off a frenzy of excitement.

For days before the date of the celebration the Boston papers carried stories about the impending Civic Feast. The great day began with the roar of cannon from the fort in the harbor. At eleven o'clock a procession representing the trades and crafts of Boston formed, as much like a similar outpouring in Paris as Puritan Boston could imagine it.

25

Two mounted couriers, the marshal of the day, and a brass band led off. Following the band came a complement of butchers and their apprentices dressed in white smocks and armed with cleavers and carving knives; they preceded a decorated wagon bearing a beribboned roasted ox that would presently provide food for the hungry marchers. To one of the ox's gilded horns was attached an American flag and to the other the French tricolor. A sign in gold letters labeled the ox a "Peace Offering to Liberty and Equality." A phalanx of Boston citizens marching behind the ox was followed by a wagonload of bread and a huge hogshead of rum punch. Other loads of bread and hogsheads of punch in the procession, having wound through the town past the houses of the governor and the French consul, at last brought up in State Street, where tables were erected for serving up the ox, bread, and punch.

Not even the children were forgotten, for each child received a cake bearing in icing the words "Liberty and Equality." The populace of Boston, every apprentice and journeyman, was invited to this feast celebrating equality. But at two o'clock another procession marched from the State House to Faneuil Hall for a more formal banquet. Some citizens of Boston were obviously more equal than others. Samuel Adams, the great firebrand of the American War of Independence, was the orator of the occasion. The hall, the so-called Cradle of American Liberty, given to Boston by Peter Faneuil, a prosperous slave trader, was decorated symbolically as befitted the occasion. Before an obelisk at the west end stood a figure of Liberty. In her left hand she bore her insignia and in her right a copy of Tom Paine's *The Rights of Man*, a book that the revolutionaries accepted as their Bible. Under Liberty's feet were the broken symbols of despotism: a crown, a scepter, a bishop's battered miter, and shattered chains. Banners and flags bedecked the hall, along with inscriptions of "Liberty and Equality" mixed here and there with other signs saying "Justice and Peace." Sam Adams made a rousing speech,

26

and the audience was so moved by goodwill and rum that they raised a purse to pay the fines of prisoners in the town jail, who were invited to join the happy throng.

After fireworks and bonfires the crowds, who had eaten the barbecued ox, drunk the hogsheads of punch, and listened to impassioned orators glorifying France, liberty, equality, and anything else that seemed appropriate, at last struggled home. Miraculously no serious fires broke out, and few republicans were injured in the crowded streets by runaway vehicles. The Boston populace had caught a glimpse of untrammeled liberty.

Not every Bostonian looked with favor on the proceedings. Some thoughtful citizens glowered at this display of popular enthusiasm for a country that they believed was plunging itself and perhaps others into ruin. In the plebeian excitement of Boston's butchers and bakers—as well as the partisanship shown by a few men of financial stature—conservatives saw trouble ahead for the American Republic. John Adams was one who looked upon it all and grumbled. He never trusted the French. Three years before this he had written to a friend in England saying, "I know not what to make of a republic of thirty million atheists"—his designation of the godless French.

The significance of the French Revolution's repeal of the Christian God and the establishment of the Goddess of Reason had not yet dawned upon Puritan New England. For example, in Plymouth, Massachusetts, on January 24, 1793, the establishment of the French Republic was celebrated with an address by the most eloquent of the local preachers, the singing of hymns, and the shouting of an "Ode to Liberty" composed on the spur of the moment by a Plymouth poet. *The Columbian Centinel* for January 30 reported that the Reverend Dr. Robins gave a "brief and connected sketch of the principles and leading events of the French Revolution" which delighted all who heard him by its "happy eloquence." The people "united with him in adopting the sublime and striking language of the Prophet

27

Daniel, 'Blessed be the name of God forever and ever: for wisdom and might are his and he changeth the times and season. He removeth Kings.' After the address Billings' 'Independence' was sung by a select choir who performed their parts with energies suited to the subject. 'Down with these earthly Kings' thundered the majestic bass. 'No King but God' was the sublime response." In a parade that followed the church service, the procession stopped here and there in the streets of Plymouth, and "at proper intervals the 'Ode to Liberty' which Citizen J. Croswell composed in a moment of happy inspiration was repeatedly sung. . . . The company retired seasonably in the afternoon satisfied with themselves, with each other, and with their country. A cheerful ball closed the enjoyment of this agreeable day."

Throughout the country, not only in the cities but in small towns and villages, people gathered to rejoice at the establishment of the French Republic. Republics were a rarity, and those Americans who remembered their classical history equated the new republics in America and France with the idealized state of republican Rome. Americans, whose minds were still filled with propaganda about the tyranny of George III, whooped and cheered over accounts of the overthrow of the King of France and the creation of a sister republic.

Even Thomas Jefferson, who had cautioned his friends in France against eliminating the monarchy, came to believe that the survival of the newly established French Republic was essential to the survival of our own form of government. If the alliance formed in Europe to suppress the French Revolution succeeded in restoring the Bourbons, he feared that reactionary forces would also destroy the American Republic.

The news of the execution of Louis XVI and his queen, Marie Antoinette, gave second thoughts to many Americans, as did the excesses of the Reign of Terror, as these reports drifted across the Atlantic. Eyewitness accounts by refugees, many of whom were attractive and persuasive, convinced many Americans that the French revolutionaries had carried their ideas of liberty to a dangerous excess.

But a few fanatical American republicans expressed open pleasure at the beheading of the French king. In fact, not until the Reign of Terror had nearly run its course in France did many enthusiasts for the Revolution over here comprehend the extent of the bloodbath that France had undergone. Charles D. Hazen, in *Contemporary American Opinion of the French Revolution*, describes a dinner in Philadelphia during the height of the Terror at which "the head of a [roasted] pig was severed from its body, and being recognized as an emblem of the murdered King of France, was carried round to the guests. 'Each one placing the cap of liberty upon its head, pronounced the word "tyrant" and proceeded to mangle with his knife the head of the luckless creature doomed to be served to so unworthy a company.' " This quotation by Hazen is taken from the *National Gazette* for July 17, 1793.[2]

Even Jefferson felt obliged to make excuses for the French execution of their king. He declared that this deed might serve to "soften the monarchical governments by rendering monarchs amenable to punishment like other criminals." He had come thus far from the time only a few years before when he had advised French reformers to retain the monarchy and model it after England's.

But the fervor of the mad and riotous celebrations of French liberty was cooling. The new American nation found itself in a dilemma. Its Treaty of Alliance with France made in 1778 required it to come to France's aid if the latter's Caribbean island possessions should be attacked. England was now at war with France and would certainly make an effort to take the French islands. Would the United States go to war with England to save France's possessions? The nation was in no condition to wage another war; furthermore, trade with England was improving, and merchants, just recovering from the recent conflict, would not tolerate its interruption.

In this crisis, President Washington on April 22, 1793, issued a Proclamation of Neutrality. With the republican enthusiasts for France the proclamation of course was unpopular, and they denounced Washington as the tool of England. Throughout the country these partisans quickly organized "Democratic Clubs" to support the French cause and combat the influence of the conservative Federalists. In every town, village, and tavern, wherever people gathered, politics provided a staple of conversation. Few Americans were so benighted that they did not have a political opinion which they were ready to express by word or demonstration.

At this juncture France chose to send to the United States an ambassador who proved to be one of the most incredible diplomatic representatives this country has ever seen, one Citizen Edmond Genêt. He arrived in Charleston, South Carolina, on April 8, 1793, where French enthusiasts received him with a rousing welcome and a gala dinner. Immediately Genêt began to issue letters of marque to privateers, which authorized them to prey on British commerce. As he slowly proceeded toward Philadelphia to present his credentials to an embarrassed Jefferson, the Secretary of State, Genêt continued to act with arrogant disregard of diplomatic propriety and to drum up support for France despite the neutral status of his host nation. He tried to organize Jacobin clubs, which today would be called Communist, and even sought to encourage land speculators and adventurers in Kentucky and Ohio to start a war against Spain on the Mississippi frontier. In short, Citizen Genêt proved such a pest that Jefferson had to ask France to recall him. Genêt had the wit not to return to France and risk his head under the guillotine; instead, he married the daughter of Governor George Clinton of New York, bought a farm, and lived out his life as a quiet citizen of the United States. Genêt's activities as ambassador further helped cool American enthusiasm for France. When a few years later, in 1798 and 1799, the French government un-

Patrick Henry was most famous for his speech to the Virginia Assembly at Richmond in 1775. The ringing words of his conclusion became the battle cry of the Revolution: "Give me liberty or give me death!" *This Currier and Ives lithograph was published for the centenary celebration of 1876. Courtesy, Library of Congress.*

leashed its warships on American shipping bound for England, friendship for a former ally turned into an undeclared war.

Politics as a subject of universal interest, indeed, as a national diversion that developed in the first years of the American Republic, continued to hold the interest of Americans from that day to this. Both local and national elections gave occasion for entertainment, excitement, occasional violence, and celebration. Americans developed an incredible appetite for political oratory, which only lately has shown signs of diminishing. From Patrick Henry to Franklin Roosevelt, listeners have been captivated by golden words.

Daniel Webster, Senator from Massachusetts, was the greatest spellbinder of the first half of the nineteenth century, and a speech by this oratorical genius drew enraptured audiences. On January 26, 1830, when he made his most famous Senatorial speech defending the idea of an indivisible union against the attacks of Senator Robert Y. Hayne of South Carolina, so many people crowded into the Capitol that the audience overflowed even into the Senate chamber itself.

A member of the audience, Margaret Bayard Smith, in her memoirs, *The First Forty Years of Washington Society*, gives a vivid description of the event:

The Senate chamber is the present arena and never were the amphitheatres of Rome more crowded by the highest ranks of both sexes than the Senate chamber is.

31

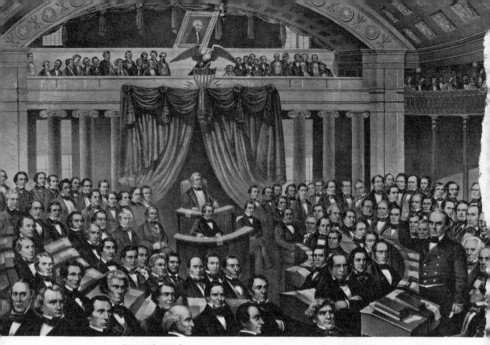

Daniel Webster's oratory drew crowds to the Senate floor and galleries for more than twenty years. He is pictured here in the great debate on the Compromise of 1850. "I speak today," he said, "for the preservation of the Union. 'Hear me for my cause.'" *Lithograph by Jones and Clark, 1860. Courtesy, Library of Congress.*

Every seat, every inch of ground, even the steps, were compactly filled, and yet not space enough for the ladies. The Senators were obliged to relinquish their chairs of state to the fair auditors who literally sat in the Senate. One lady sat in Col. Hayne's seat, while he stood by her side speaking. I cannot but regret that this dignified body should become such a scene of personality and popular resort. It was supposed yesterday that there were 300 ladies besides their attendant beaux on the floor of the Senate. The two galleries were crowded to overflowing with *the People*. . . . Our government is becoming every day more and more democratic; the rulers of the people are truly their servants and among those rulers women are gaining more than their share of power.[3]

Webster on this occasion spoke for hours to an audience who sat or stood entranced. The conclusion of his speech—an oration in itself—ended with the words "Liberty and Union, now and forever, one and inseparable." This part of Webster's speech, printed over and over, became a favorite oration for schoolboys, who liked to thunder it out on Friday afternoons—the conventional day for oratorical recitations in schools.

Presidential campaigns and inaugurations from early times provided excitement and diversion. The height of public participation in an inauguration was reached when President Andrew Jackson, favorably known in the back country for his toughness as Old Hickory, took office on March 4, 1829. Nothing like the swarms of all sorts and conditions of people ever before had been seen in the little capital of Washington. They came through the mud on foot, on horseback, in wagons, or in carriages. Jackson himself plodded up muddy Pennsylvania Avenue to the Capitol to take the oath of office. After he had managed to push through the crowd, he rode a horse back to the President's House, as the White House was then called, followed by the whole crowd, all of whom were welcome to come to the "reception." The crush very nearly suffocated Jackson, who was finally rescued by a body of friends who stood like football tackles bucking the crowd. Only the word that bar-

President-elect Andrew Jackson made his "whistle stops" by stagecoach en route to Washington for his inauguration in 1829. *Engraving after Howard Pyle in* Harper's Weekly, *March 12, 1881. Courtesy, Library of Congress.*

rels of whiskey and punch were open on the grounds outside drained off the crowd. But already men and boys in hobnailed and muddy boots, standing on chairs and the piano to get a glimpse of Old Hickory, had ruined the furniture. The floor was a litter of broken glasses, cups, and dishes; spilled punch sloshed about the floors. Mrs. Smith describes the swarms of people:

Country men, farmers, gentlemen, mounted and dismounted, boys, women and children, black and white. Carriages, wagons, carts all pursuing him to the President's house. . . . [Mrs. Smith's party had to wait because of the jam but eventually got in.] Some one came and informed us the crowd before the President's house was so far lessened that they thought we might enter. This time we effected our purpose. But what a scene did we witness! The *Majesty of the People* had disappeared, and a rabble, a mob, of boys, Negroes, women, children, scrambling, fighting, romping. What a pity, what a pity! No arrangements had been made, no police officers placed on duty, and the whole house had been inundated by the rabble mob. We came too late. The President, after having been *literally* nearly pressed to death and almost suffocated and torn to pieces by the people in their eagerness to shake hands with Old Hickory, had retreated through the back way or south front and had escaped to his lodgings at Gadsby's. Cut glass and china in the amount of several thousand dollars had been broken in the struggle to get the refreshments; punch and other articles had

Major General Andrew Jackson, nicknamed Old Hickory by his troops in the War of 1812, rode to the White House largely on his popularity as a military hero. *Engraving by Longacre after the portrait by Thomas Sully.* Courtesy, Library of Congress.

been carried out in tubs and buckets, but had it been in hogsheads, it would have been insufficient ice-creams, and cake, and lemonade for 20,000 people, for it is said that number were there, tho' I think the estimate exaggerated. Ladies fainted; men were seen with bloody noses, and such a scene of confusion took place as is impossible to describe. Those who got in could not get out by the door again but had to scramble out of windows. . . . But it was the People's day, and the People's President, and the People would rule. God grant that one day or other the People do not put down all rule and rulers. I fear, enlightened Freemen as they are, they will be found, as they have been found in all ages and countries where they get the power in their hands, that of all tyrants, they are the most ferocious, cruel, and despotic.[4]

Although the writer of these memoirs was herself an ardent Democrat and a worshiper of Thomas Jefferson, she, like others, recalled the Reign of Terror in France and was fearful of an overdose of democracy in America. But no one could deny that the populace had enjoyed a rousing celebration at Old Hickory's inauguration, however much their heads might ache the day after.

If anything, the entertainment provided by politics increased during the next two decades. For example, the campaign of 1840 is described by Commager and Morison in *The Growth of the American Republic* as "the jolliest presidential election America has ever seen."[5] The Whigs (who roughly corresponded to modern Republicans) nominated for President General William Henry Harrison, hero of the Battle of Tippecanoe over the Indians; for Vice President the nominee was John Tyler. The Democrats renominated President Martin Van Buren. A comment by a Democratic newspaper that instead of the Presidency, all Harrison needed was a log cabin with plenty of hard cider to drink resulted in a rousing "log-cabin" campaign. Although

The "log-cabin campaign" of 1840 portrayed General Harrison as a farmer, with log cabin and cider barrel as his symbols. Contemporary campaign broadsides. Courtesy, Library of Congress.

Harrison was a substantial citizen with a large house in Ohio, he was pictured as a rustic in coonskin cap, fresh from his log cabin on the frontier. The Whigs pictured President Van Buren, whom they blamed for the panic and economic depression of 1837, as an effete aristocrat from the East who perfumed his whiskers with cologne and spent his time sipping champagne from a cut-glass goblet. Ironically the Democrats, who had capitalized in Jackson's campaign on their reputation as the "party of the People," now found themselves outmaneuvered by the Whigs, who had appropriated their propaganda. The Whigs went about with log-cabin badges, dispensing hard cider and boasting about their candidates' concern for the people. One of their campaign songs reminded the populace of Harrison's prowess

36

against the Indians. Its chorus began, "Tippecanoe and Tyler too." The Democrats enviously charged that the Whigs won friends by spiking cider at their rallies with whiskey, but they found no way to counteract the "democratic" bunkum dispensed by their opponents. Everybody had a good time except poor Van Buren and his party faithfuls, and the Whigs won by a four-to-one majority. Unhappily for the Whigs, however, General Harrison died after a month in office, and Tyler, who really was more Democrat at heart than Whig, took office.

In the days before television, motion pictures, and picture magazines, we can imagine the entertainment that political campaigns on all levels gave the public. Parades, torchlight processions, picnics and barbecues, and the endless oratory of the candidates provided infinite enjoyment for the electorate and perhaps supplied a modicum of political enlightenment.

The lordly *Constitution*, "laying to, unbending sails, repairing her rigging," surveys another victim, the British ship *Java*, sunk on the evening of December 29, 1812. Some twenty years later, when the great ship was threatened with demolition, Oliver Wendell Holmes' poem "Old Ironsides" recalled the days of her glory:

> Her deck, once red with heroes' blood,
>   Where knelt the vanquished foe,
> When winds were hurrying o'er the flood,
>   And waves were white below,
> No more shall feel the victor's tread,
>   Or know the conquered knee;—
> The harpies of the shore shall pluck
>   The eagle of the sea!

Saved for posterity, Old Ironsides remains docked at Boston as a national monument. *Engraving by R. & D. Havell after a sketch by Lieutenant Buchanan. Courtesy, Eleutherian Mills Historical Library.*

Chapter 3

Hardships and Problems of the Early Years

Although Americans in the early years of the Republic might revel in their newly won freedom from the rule of George III, their lot for the first two decades after the War of Independence was far from easy. Wars inevitably disrupt the normal routines of life, and the American Revolution had brought disasters to various parts of the country. Not only had some regions been overrun and despoiled by armies, but the war had engendered bitter animosity between loyalists opposed to the war (called Tories) and the patriots.

Many Americans had been opposed to breaking the ties with Great Britain, and even after the fateful decision was made on July 4, 1776, every colony had important citizens who disapproved of the action. During the war that followed, more than 70,000 loyalists left the thirteen colonies. Most went to Canada, but some crossed the Atlantic to England. Loyalists were particularly numerous in Pennsylvania and the Carolinas. When the British were in possession of Philadelphia, prominent families entertained the officers and enjoyed a fashionable social life while Washington and his ragged troops were spending a bleak and desperate winter at Valley Forge. Tories in July, 1778, led a party of Mohawk Indians in an attack on settlers in the Wyoming Valley of northeastern Pennsylvania and joined in the bloody massacre that followed. In November of the same year Tories instigated a similar Indian raid on Cherry Valley in upper New York State where they slaughtered men, women, and children.

Historians have estimated that throughout the colonies a third of the population sympathized with Great Britain. As an indication of the strength of the Tories, New York alone furnished the British army with 15,000 men. In South Carolina the Tories were particularly strong in the upper part of the state, and in many communities neighbor fought against neighbor in the bitterest of partisan warfare.

Where patriots were strong enough to enforce their wills they penalized the Tories by both legal and illegal means. Those who would not take the oath of allegiance to the new nation were disfranchised and could not vote or carry a case to court. Some had their property confiscated. Here and there mobs tarred and feathered Tories and rode them out of town on a rail; they were lucky to escape with their lives.

When the war was over, patriots did not forget the role of the Tories. Although the states made an effort at reconcilia-

Tarring and feathering was a favorite form of punishment by rioters in the eighteenth century—and later. This view shows an English interpretation of the hostility of Bostonians to the tea tax, the Stamp Act, and royal tax collectors. *First published in London shortly after the "Boston Tea Party" of December 16, 1773, the cartoon was reproduced in this lithograph by Pendleton at Boston in 1830. Courtesy, Library of Congress.*

tion by passing laws to restore confiscated property, the laws were not always enforced with justice. Tories known to have participated in attacks on their neighbors risked their lives if they returned to their former communities. Many years would pass before the bitterness produced by the war would fade.

In the meantime other problems plagued the ordinary citizen attempting to resume the normal course of his life. Nearly everyone worried about taxes, debts, and inflation, the perennial concerns of mankind. Seven states issued quantities of paper money and required creditors to accept it in payment of debts. Since the money quickly depreciated, some creditors went into hiding to avoid being paid off in worthless paper money. A depression that held the country in its grip for several years ruined many businessmen and caused much grumbling and distress. Money was scarce and jobs were few. Many skilled craftsmen were unable to find work, for even the well-to-do could not raise the cash to pay wages for needed work. No one had ever heard of unemployment insurance or welfare as we know it. The poor, who had not yet learned to depend on organized government help, shifted for themselves as best they could.

But hard as times were, conditions were less desperate than in an urbanized society. The majority of the population still lived on the land, on farms, where they raised most of the necessities of life. No farmers were so lazy that they faced starvation. They raised their own corn and wheat, which they ground at a local mill. Their cows found their own living in grassy pastures and provided ample milk and butter. Pigs, sheep, and calves furnished meat, which a farmer could salt down or pickle in brine for future use. Chickens, ducks, geese, and turkeys were abundant. In the north the sap of maple trees was boiled down into sugar and molasses. Coffee and tea were the most expensive luxuries that required a cash outlay. But many a countryman made do with herb and sassafras tea.

Even most townsmen had vegetable gardens and usually

41

kept a cow, which was led to pasture each morning. Tastes were simpler in these times, and luxuries were fewer. No frozen or expensively packaged foods in supermarkets tempted the purses of our ancestors, for these did not exist. Housewives shelled peas or strung beans picked in their own gardens. In the winter few vegetables graced the dinner table, and these were such as would keep in the cellar: turnips, cabbage, sauerkraut, and potatoes. Apple cider, both sweet and hard, was a favorite drink. Though everywhere men might complain, none would perish.

Even if land was fertile and crops bountiful, farmers found it difficult to translate their produce into hard money. The stable markets that had existed before the war were in disarray. Great Britain had been the colonies' best customer, but now much of the British market, including the British islands in the Caribbean, was closed to American trade.

Farmers and trappers in the backcountry of Kentucky and Ohio suffered from lack of transportation to Eastern markets. No adequate roads led across the mountains, and their best market was New Orleans and other towns on the lower Mississippi, then held by the Spaniards. It was easier to float wheat, corn, salt pork, furs, and other products down the Ohio and the Mississippi to New Orleans and ship them by sea to Eastern ports of the United States than to try to move them over the mountains by packtrains. But the Spaniards in control of the mouth of the Mississippi were not always cooperative. From time to time they closed the port of New Orleans, and that threat was constantly in the minds of Americans interested in Western development.

One product, however, that was valuable and relatively easy to transport was whiskey. Large quantities of corn and rye produced west of the Alleghenies, especially in western Pennsylvania, were thus reduced in bulk at distilleries which many farmers operated. In the West whiskey virtually became legal tender, as tobacco had been in Virginia in the colonial period. Men bartered whiskey at country stores for other products, and churches even paid part of their preachers' salaries in whiskey. Consequently, when Alexander Hamilton, Secretary of the Treasury, in 1791 pushed through Congress an excise tax on whiskey, the new revenue act created intense anger in whiskey-making regions. Three years later a similar excise tax was placed on snuff and loaf sugar.

The whiskey tax stirred up violent controversy. Although reformers here and there preached against the abuse of whiskey, most of the country regarded it as a necessity. On the frontier someone declared that a barrel of whiskey a week was "but a small allowance for a large family without a cow." When the College of Physicians in Philadelphia issued a statement that too much whiskey drinking was bad for the health, General James Jackson of Georgia, defending in Congress the rights of his constituents, declared that "they have been long in the habit of getting drunk and that they will get drunk in defiance of a dozen colleges or all the excise duties which Congress might be weak or wicked enough to impose."[1]

Drunk or sober, Westerners decided to oppose the tax with force if necessary, and the summer of 1794 found the four western counties of Pennsylvania in open revolt. Rebels burned the house of General John Neville, the excise inspector, abused tax collectors, and threatened to march on Pittsburgh and even to continue on to Philadelphia.

So great was the threat to the security of the country that President Washington called for volunteers to suppress the rebellion. Nearly 13,000 men responded, and the President himself took the field for a time. Portions of this unwieldy army marched west but found no rebels eager to fight. After arresting twenty nondescripts and marching them through the streets of Philadelphia, they imprisoned them for a few months. Only two were convicted of treason, and both were later pardoned by the President, one because he was crazy, and the other because he was described as a "simpleton."

Thus ended the great "Whiskey Rebellion" that for a season created vast excitement throughout the country.

At the beginning of the War of Independence many Americans, both North and South, owed money to their agents and merchants in Great Britain. The collection of these debts proved a sore point after the war. Some Americans wanted to repudiate the debts altogether and refuse payment, an act that threatened a new war with Great Britain. Secretary Hamilton stood firmly for payment of the debts as essential to the maintenance of the credit of the United States. But many pro-French sympathizers were still so anti-British that they wanted to refuse to allow British merchants to collect their debts. In this way they would seek revenge for Great Britain's refusal to allow free trade with its possessions. Anti-British factions openly talked of war, though the country had no standing army and no navy.

American merchants attempting to trade with Portugal, Spain, and other Mediterranean countries encountered another difficulty. Pirates from the Barbary coast of North Africa, especially from Algeria, formerly restrained by the British navy, now freely attacked American ships; the pirates even sailed beyond Gibraltar and captured American ships in the Atlantic and made slaves of their crews. Americans believed that the British encouraged them to prey on commerce competing with the British or aiding Britain's enemies. Since the Americans had sold off their last naval vessel at the end of the War of Independence and now had no navy, James Madison of Virginia proposed that they hire the Portuguese navy to protect American shipping. Another Virginian in the House of Representatives, William B. Giles, argued against creating a navy because he "considered navies altogether as very foolish things,"[2] a reason for exorbitant taxes. Americans on the frontiers, suffering from Indian attacks, also blamed the British, for Britain still held outposts in the borderland. Officers at these forts, it was charged, incited the Indians to attack

Americans and encouraged them to believe that Great Britain would soon reclaim territories won by the Americans in the last war.

Anti-British sentiment was so strong that President Washington determined to try to negotiate a more favorable treaty with Great Britain that would relieve some of the tension. To deal with the British and arrange a treaty, Washington in the summer of 1794 appointed Chief Justice John Jay as minister plenipotentiary. Jay found British officials unyielding on many points but managed to wring from them a few favorable terms and agreed to a treaty which, with a few alterations, the Senate ratified on June 24, 1795.

This treaty was violently denounced by the Republicans who called it a sellout to Great Britain. The British had refused to abandon the doctrine of the right of search of neutral ships in time of war for contraband stores intended for the enemy—a cause of future friction and conflict—but they had made useful trade concessions, agreed to evacuate forts on the American frontier, to cease inciting the Indians, and to adjudicate claims for war damages. The United States guaranteed the payments of prewar debts owing British subjects. Though the treaty was widely denounced, within five years after its ratification American trade had increased 300 percent, and Americans were once more shipping foodstuffs and other products to the West Indies, a profitable market. The treaty had also opened British India to American traders, marking the beginning of a long commerce with Asia.

Even though business improved after the ratification of Jay's Treaty, Republicans continued their attacks on the pro-British policies of the government. When Washington declined to run for a third term as President, the Republicans might have succeeded in electing Jefferson in 1796 if the French minister to the United States had not openly campaigned for him and thus alienated voters who objected to such foreign meddling. As it was, John Adams, a crusty

45

Federalist who heartily distrusted France, was elected. Under the system then in use, Jefferson, as the runner-up, was named Vice President. The French attack on American shipping bound for England and the English possessions in 1798 and 1799 caused further dislike of France and resulted in an official war at sea that stirred American patriotism. For by this time Congress had created a little navy; by 1800 it had fourteen men-of-war at sea. When Captain Thomas Truxton in the *Constellation* in 1799 captured the French frigate *L'Insurgente*, even some diehard Republicans cheered.

Fear of open war with France—and of the disloyalty of pro-French Americans—reached a point of hysteria in 1798 and 1799. Federalist propagandists declared that France was intent upon usurping American liberties and making the United States a godless satellite of its own godless government. Years before, John Adams had expressed his own concern over that "nation of atheists," and time had not altered his views. But some Federalist members of Congress were more violently concerned about France than Adams and other members of his administration. Many believed that war with France was imminent and that laws were needed to curb dangerous traitors at home. French sympathizers were labeled Jacobins—that is, in today's language, Communists. Hysterical newspapers declared that they were ready to turn the country over to a rabble of foreign atheists who would dethrone God, bring on anarchy, and countenance free love and every form of vice.

Frightened by a prospect so dreadful, the Federalists in the summer of 1798 rushed through Congress four acts called collectively the Alien and Sedition Acts. One act was aimed at curbing immigration and the naturalization of aliens. For citizenship it extended the necessary period of residency in the country from five to fourteen years. Refugees had come from various countries of Europe, and most of these immigrants had joined the Republican Party. The Federalists raised a specter of foreigners thus gaining control of the government, foreigners of whom they did not approve. One Federalist Senator, after touring Pennsylvania, reported with horror seeing large numbers of "United Irishmen, Free Masons, and the most God-provoking democrats this side of hell."[3] In Federalist eyes, to be a democrat was to be little better than one of the wicked.

The Sedition Acts were designed to curb conspiracies against the government and to prevent the writing, speaking, or publishing of anything "false, scandalous, and malicious" against the government or any government official. This was a clear attack on freedom of speech and freedom of the press, but it passed Congress as necessary in case of war with France. A few editors were convicted, fined, and jailed under this law. One of the victims was Matthew Lyon of Vermont, who was jailed in the summer of 1798 for publishing in the *Vermont Journal* an attack on President Adams. The injustice of his trial and his subsequent shoddy treatment made him such a martyr and hero that he was elected to Congress from the jail. A little later, by a curious irony of fate, Lyon cast one of the two deciding votes that made Jefferson President when that election was thrown into the House of Representatives for decision.

The Alien and Sedition Acts, passed as emergency measures to run for a definite term, did not long survive, but they served one purpose unforeseen by the Federalists. They united the Republicans into a solid democratic bloc and helped ensure Jefferson's election to the Presidency in 1800. The campaign was one of the bitterest in American history. Jefferson's enemies called him every evil name in the dictionary and accused him of every iniquity that imagination could conjure up. When the electoral votes were counted, Jefferson and Aaron Burr tied for first place, and President Adams placed third. In this situation the Constitution provided for the House of Representatives to decide, and Jefferson was finally elected by two votes after a prolonged deadlock and much political bickering. Burr became Vice President. John Adams was so angry over his defeat that he rode out of Washington without waiting for his rival's inauguration.

Jefferson's election represented a victory for the common man, and there was widespread rejoicing among ordinary people everywhere. Some thought that their troubles were over and that a friend in the President's House would mean instant prosperity, for such is the delusion with which voters are hypnotized in all ages. The defeated Federalists cried ruin and declared that the ship of state was on the rocks. But the nation survived, and many great things were done, though Jefferson could neither unite all the country nor ensure prosperity. Troubles that beset his predecessors outlasted his two administrations and remained acute for many years.

Even one of Jefferson's greatest accomplishments, the purchase of Louisiana, a territory that made possible the expansion of the United States ultimately to the Pacific, almost caused the secession of New England. The conservatives of the Northeast were horrified at the thought of taking in wild fanatics from the West, some of them Frenchmen, who would create a radical majority and bring disaster to decent people. Massachusetts threatened to withdraw from the Union rather than share it with wild men but ultimately thought better of it.

The purchase of Louisiana was the greatest real estate bargain in history. France had ceded it to Spain in 1763 to keep it from falling into England's hands at the end of the Seven Years' War, but Napoleon had forced Spain to return it to France by the secret Treaty of San Ildefonso on October 1, 1800. Disturbed at the prospect of the port of New Orleans being closed to American goods coming down the Ohio and Mississippi rivers, Jefferson declared that "the day that France takes possession of New Orleans . . . we must marry ourselves to the British fleet and nation." But he preferred to buy the port if possible. To this end he sent agents to France to negotiate with Napoleon. Bonaparte realized that once more England might take Louisiana, so

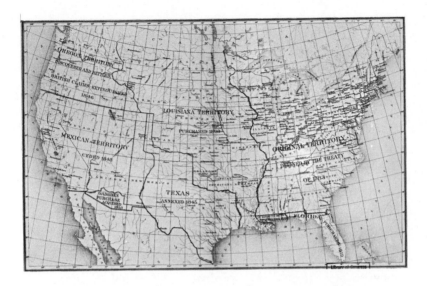

The Louisiana Territory, purchased by President Jefferson from Napoleon in 1803, brought to the Union the vast heartland between the Mississippi and the Rockies, Canada and the Gulf of Mexico. The way was open for westward expansion, and just fifty years later the new nation stretched "from sea to shining sea." *Map printed by J. Bien & Co., for the U.S. Bureau of the Census, 1901. Courtesy, Library of Congress.*

he agreed to sell not only New Orleans but the whole of the territory to the United States for 60,000,000 francs (approximately $12,000,000). The deal was closed on April 30, 1803. Even before this, Jefferson had obtained authorization from Congress to send an exploring party across the continent to the Pacific; this was the famous expedition led by Meriwether Lewis and William Clark.

Though a man of peace, Jefferson decided that only force would end the capture and enslavement of American seamen by the Barbary pirates. On May 14, 1801, the Pasha of Tripoli ordered his soldiers to chop down the flagpole in front of the American consulate as token of his declaration of war because of American failure to satisfy

49

his greed. But Jefferson had already ordered warships to the Mediterranean, and for the next four years the little navy carried on a brave but desultory war against the pirates. Finally in 1805 Tripoli was forced to make a satisfactory treaty. It was in this war that William Eaton led a rabble army, reinforced by Lieutenant Presley N. O'Bannon and seven marines, to capture the Tripolitan city of Derna. This episode gave the United States Marines the phrase in their hymn "to the shores of Tripoli."

During Jefferson's second administration his former Vice President, Aaron Burr, conceived a visionary plot of setting up an independent republic in the West. Precisely what he planned has never been clear, but he persuaded the British minister that for $500,000 he could get the Western states to secede from the Union. A bit later he dazzled an Irishman named Harman Blennerhasset, who had established

Participating in a naval blockade of Tripoli during the Barbary Wars, the U.S. frigate *Philadelphia* ran aground and was captured by the Tripolitans. Refloated and anchored under the harbor guns of the enemy, she was boarded, recaptured, and burned on the night of February 16, 1804, in a daring exploit led by Stephen Decatur. *Engraving by John B. Guerrazzi, 1805. Courtesy, Library of Congress.*

In the fight for the *Philadelphia* another hero's name was added to the early annals of the U.S. Navy. At the height of the fray a sailor, mistakenly identified as Reuben James, thrust his own head between an Algerian sword and Decatur, thus giving his life for his commander's. A U.S. destroyer named for Reuben James was sunk in the North Atlantic on October 30, 1941, by a German submarine. *Engraving published by Johnson, Frye & Co., 1857, after a painting by Chappel. Courtesy, Library of Congress.*

himself on an island in the Ohio River, with a plan to invade Mexico and make himself emperor. With General James Wilkinson, then governor of Upper Louisiana and a consummate scoundrel, he plotted something or other, but Wilkinson betrayed him. The Western region was disgruntled over its fancied neglect by the Eastern states, and many restless adventurers in the Mississippi Valley were sympathetic to notions of independence.

In the summer of 1806 Burr started down the Mississippi with some sixty armed men. Just what he intended to do no one knows. Rumors of his conspiracy had already reached Washington, and the government had Burr arrested and brought to trial in Richmond, Virginia, on charges of treason. Chief Justice John Marshall, no friend of Jefferson's, who presided at the trial, so defined the law of treason that Burr was found innocent. The trial attracted immense interest, and Marshall's strict interpretation of the constitutional definition of treason as "levying war against the United States or adhering to their enemies," with the provision that there must be "two witnesses to the same overt act," established a precedent that influenced all later treason trials.

51

The most worrisome problems during Jefferson's second administration resulted from the Napoleonic Wars, when both France and England interfered with American ships in an effort to blockade each other. England's success in the conflict with Napoleon depended upon its command of the seas and the effectiveness of the British navy. It insisted upon searching American vessels for deserters from English ships and the impressment of English subjects found in American ships. Not always were English search parties careful to distinguish between American and British sailors when the English needed crews. Jefferson lodged vigorous protests against the policy of search and impressment.

The two countries narrowly avoided war in the summer of 1807, when a British man-of-war, the *Leopard*, overhauled an American war vessel, the *Chesapeake*, off the Virginia coast. When the *Chesapeake*'s captain refused to permit his vessel to be searched, the *Leopard* opened fire and killed three men and wounded a number of others. The incident caused a fever of war sentiment in the country, despite the fact that the British apologized and offered indemnities.

In an effort to stave off war and to protect American ships, Jefferson persuaded Congress in December, 1807, to pass the Embargo Act that cut off all trade with Europe. American ships could not sail to foreign ports, and the export of goods to Europe was forbidden. Even the import of some English goods was made illegal. The intention of the act was to starve out England until it gave up the search of American ships on the high seas. But the law had no such effect. Instead, it nearly starved American workers, precipitated a grim depression, and caused New England to threaten secession from the Union. Three days before Jefferson's term as President expired he signed into law an act repealing the embargo. In the meantime many American sailors and workers in the shipyards of the country had gone to Canada to seek jobs. Times were hard, and everybody complained.

Jefferson's successor in the Presidency, James Madison of Virginia, inherited all the problems of the previous administration and was unable to keep the country from drifting into war with Great Britain. Not only was the country angered by British interference with American shipping, but frontiersmen in the Northwest were itching to invade and seize Canada. The Westerners were convinced that British agents from Canada were responsible for stirring up Indian forays on American settlements. So, on June 18, 1812, Congress passed a resolution declaring war on Great Britain.

Few wars in history have been so incompetently fought by both antagonists, and few have accomplished so little. The United States had only a tiny regular army and had to depend on hastily called militia without training. Most of its officers were incompetents left over from the Revolution. The British were still too busy fighting Napoleon to bother with America. The American militiamen frequently refused to fight or to obey orders of their officers. The Americans

"The Taking of the City of Washington in America"—a British version of the burning of the capital on August 24, 1814. "With the flotilla, the public property destroyed amounted to thirty million of dollars." *Engraving published by G. Thompson, London, in October, 1814. Courtesy, Library of Congress.*

A view of the Capitol Building as it appeared after the burning of Washington by the British in 1814. *Aquatint by W. Strickland after G. Munger. Courtesy, Library of Congress.*

managed to make a brief advance into Canada and to burn York, later known as Toronto, then the capital of Canada, an act that caused the British later to retaliate and burn Washington.

On August 24, 1814, a British force commanded by General Robert Ross and Admiral George Cockburn, which had marched up the banks of the Patuxent River, routed a militia army of 7,000 men at Bladensburg, not far from Washington, and advanced on the American capital. They got there in time to eat a dinner prepared at the White House for President Madison, who had discreetly fled into Virginia. The British then burned the White House, the Capitol, and other public buildings but forbade any looting of private houses. Mrs. Margaret Bayard Smith in her memoirs wrote despondently of the plight of the capital: "I do not suppose Government will ever return to Washington."[4]

Another stirring incident of the War of 1812 was the twenty-five-hour bombardment by the British fleet of Fort McHenry, gateway to Baltimore, through the day and night of September 3, 1814. By dawn's early light on the fourteenth, Francis Scott Key, a Washington lawyer held prisoner on one of the warships, strained through smoke and haze to see that the flag over the fort was still there. He then started to write, on the back of a letter, "The Star-Spangled Banner." *Aquatint by J. Bower. Courtesy, Library of Congress.*

The war finally drew to an inconclusive end, and commissioners of Great Britain and the United States signed a treaty of peace at Ghent on Christmas Eve, 1814. News of the peace did not reach the United States in time to prevent the Battle of New Orleans on January 8, 1815. General Andrew Jackson with 3,500 riflemen safe behind breastworks of mud, cotton bales, and sugar barrels poured a deadly fire into the 5,300 British veterans of the Napoleonic Wars led by General Sir Edward Pakenham. The British leader was killed in the first onslaught, and the two generals

American victories at sea in the War of 1812 contributed to a growing naval tradition, especially the exploits of the heavy frigate *Constitution*. First and most important of these was her engagement on August 19, 1812, with the British frigate *Guerrière*, in which she earned the nickname "Old Ironsides." *Engraving by C. Tiebout, 1813, after T. Birch. Courtesy, Library of Congress.*

next in command were fatally wounded. Two thousand of their troops were killed or wounded in that deadly fusillade. Jackson's casualties were thirteen men killed and fifty-eight wounded. Although the British retained their position facing Jackson's riflemen for ten days, the last surviving general finally led his men aboard their transports and sailed away. This useless victory, won after peace had been made, at least made Jackson a national hero and propelled him into the Presidency in 1828.

It had been an inglorious war with only a few heroic incidents for schoolchildren to remember: for example,

Captain Stephen Decatur's capture of the British frigate *Macedonian*, two or three other naval victories, and the ineffective British bombardment of Fort McHenry guarding Baltimore, which inspired Francis Scott Key to compose our national anthem, "The Star-Spangled Banner." But though the War of 1812–15 settled few issues directly, perhaps it proved the ineffectiveness of war as a means of establishing stable relations with foreign powers. At any rate, after 1815 international problems became less acute, and the country could concentrate on developments at home.

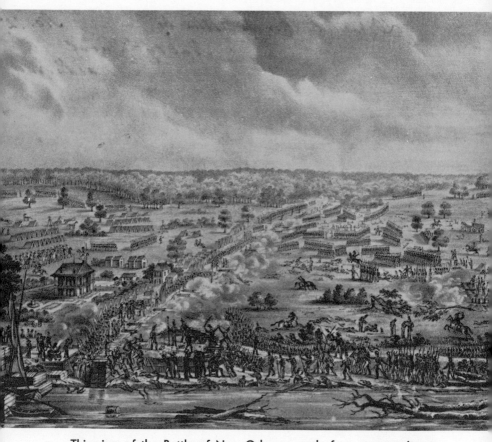

This view of the Battle of New Orleans, made from an eyewitness sketch, shows initial casualties of the British, attacking from the right and the strongly entrenched position of Andrew Jackson's defenders. Fought on January 8, 1815, two weeks after the War of 1812 had officially ended, the chief effect of this belated American victory was to propel General Jackson into the Presidency in 1828. *Lithograph by P. S. Duval, 1840, after H. Ladotte. Courtesy, Library of Congress.*

Chapter 4

Democratic "Society" and Manners

Foreign visitors to the new United States were generally critical of the manners displayed by Americans. By European standards American behavior was often considered crude and unpolished. Although Boston, Philadelphia, Charleston, and a few other cities had developed a social aristocracy in the colonial period, and many planters in Virginia and Maryland lived in baronial style, zeal for "democracy" and enthusiasm for the equality and fraternity proclaimed by the revolutionary French made aristocratic pretensions exceedingly unpopular after the War of Independence. Even President Washington was severely criticized for the formality which he insisted upon at social functions. His enemies declared that he drove around New York (the first capital of the nation) in a coach with six horses like King George himself, and his receptions (called levees and drawing rooms) smacked, they thought, of royalty.

The question of titles bothered the citizens of the new republic. A great wrangle occurred over what to call the President. John Adams and other conservative Federalists

"Lady" Washington stands regally on a dais to receive guests at one of her Friday evening "levees." Though criticized by some for excessive formality, they were the most prestigious social events of Philadelphia, the nation's capital from 1790 to 1800. *Engraving by A. H. Ritchie, 1861, after D. Huntington. Courtesy, Library of Congress.*

thought the plain term "President" not sufficiently honorific and proposed various other titles including "Excellency," "Highness," "Serene Highness," and "High Mightiness." A few even wanted to crown Washington as "King George I." In the end all these were rejected as fantasies, and the chief executive became "Mr. President" and has so remained.

But the fear of titles' becoming established was very real, and Jeffersonian republicans inveighed against the use of any terms of honor. When the Society of the Cincinnati was established in 1783 to include officers in the Continental Army, with the provision that the eldest male descendant in succession should inherit membership, a great outcry was raised; clearly this was the first step in the creation of a hereditary form of nobility. The Declaration of Independence had declared all men free and equal, and no society of aristocrats was going to change that, the republicans cried. Although Americans have shown an enduring weakness for military titles, particularly the designation "Colonel," democracy ruled out anything resembling titles of nobility. For a time French enthusiasts tried to abolish even such titles as "Mr." and "Mrs." and substitute "Citizen" and "Citess" in imitation of the revolutionary French. But that fad soon passed.

Despite the complaints and opposition of those who feared the establishment of an aristocratic tradition, a society of considerable pomp and circumstance developed around President Washington, especially after the capital moved from New York to Philadelphia. For many years Philadelphia, the largest and most prosperous city in the United States, had had an upper class of wealthy merchants and cultivated men and women. Such people naturally cut an important figure in the new government and the social circles connected with it. The President's wife was addressed as "Lady Washington," and the functions at the executive mansion were conducted with great formality.

President John Adams, who succeeded Washington, was even more conscious of his Presidential dignity, and his receptions were among the stuffiest the Republic has seen. It was in the last year of his administration that the capital was moved to Washington, and it was given to him and his wife, Abigail, to inaugurate Washington society with a New Year's Day reception at the brand-new White House in 1801. Both the President and his wife were sticklers for formality. Instead of shaking hands at his receptions, John Adams bowed stiffly. His wife, who had been presented at court when her husband was minister to Great Britain, sought to introduce the conventional manners of English court society to Presidential receptions.

Entertaining in the President's House (the White House) had its problems in the early days. The building was not complete when John Adams moved in, and only six rooms were ready for occupancy; even these were so freshly plastered that they were still damp and smelled of lime. The only heat was from fireplaces, and Mrs. Adams complained that not enough wood was supplied to keep all the fires going. No fences had yet been erected to keep out people or straying animals from the White House grounds.

Washington itself was a raw and unkempt village, with roads that were seas of mud in wet weather and ankle-deep in dust during times of drought. The capital as yet had no paved sidewalks, and some walkways were not even graveled to protect pedestrians from sliding on the treacherous mud. President Harry Truman had a story of early Washington which he was fond of telling. On the way down the hill from the Capitol one night Senator Daniel Webster, somewhat unsteady from too much drink, slipped in the mud and fell in the ditch. His companion and colleague Henry Clay tried to help him up but slipped in with him. "Dan'l," Clay said, "if I can't help you up, I can lie down with you." President Truman commented that in politics that was known as "moral support."

Many Senators and Congressmen came to the capital without their families and lived in boardinghouses along Pennsylvania Avenue or in the region east of the Capitol where land speculators were busily selling lots and telling customers that the fashionable part of the city would develop there. For a time Capitol Hill was the most favored section of Washington. Far to the west lay Georgetown, which had been a port on the Potomac for many years. The region west of the White House, now the lower end of Constitution Avenue, was a reedy swamp. A little later a canal between the Potomac and Anacostia, running along the future site of Constitution Avenue, would help drain the swamp and serve as a receptacle for offal from butcher shops in the nearby town market.

Foreign diplomats sent to the new capital of the United States were appalled by the primitive conditions of the town and by the society represented therein, although a few sportsmen among them were pleased to be able to shoot quail in sight of the Capitol. A British diplomat, Augustus John Foster, who kept a journal of his stay in Washington during Jefferson's administration, observed so many sturgeon in the Potomac near Little Falls that he had his serving man catch a large number and cure the roe into caviar. Unhappily, Foster served the caviar at a reception for Senators and Congressmen who thought it was black raspberry jam until they got it in their mouths. "Very few of them liked it but spit it out very unceremoniously as a thing excessively nasty," Foster noted.[1]

When Thomas Jefferson became President in March, 1801, he introduced a new note of informality to social functions in Washington. In fact, his efforts to emphasize the simplicity of manners desirable in a republic proved so revolutionary that he gravely offended Old World diplomats accustomed to well-defined protocol. At dinner parties at the White House, for example, the seating arrangement followed what Jefferson chose to call the "pell-mell" system. That is, a guest took in the lady who happened to be nearest him when dinner was announced and sat at any place that might be vacant. The British minister, Anthony Merry, a pompous man with an even more pompous wife, was so shocked at this affront to his diplomatic dignity that he refused to accept any more of Jefferson's invitations. But nothing shook President Jefferson's resolve to maintain his republican simplicity. Some foreign diplomats, calling at the White House, were astonished to have the front door opened by the President himself, and Senators calling were not surprised at being met by the President dressed in old clothes and carpet slippers "with his toes out."

Diplomats from abroad found the simplicity of republican manners puzzling. When President Jefferson let his young grandson run about barefooted in summer, Englishmen muttered over such behavior. Augustus John Foster, for example, commented in his journal that "Mr. Jefferson, although from his love of nature and simplicity allowed his grandson, young Randolph, to come to tea and fruit of an evening with naked legs and feet, took care to order him to have them well washed."[2]

63

Although the little Federal City of Washington was hardly more than a village in a swamp in the early days, it set the social tone of the new nation. Augustus John Foster has to admit that even though the discomforts of Washington were many, it was the most interesting place in the United States. As a young man, he was charmed with the beauty of the women who flocked to the town, where they were so vastly outnumbered by the men that their marriage opportunities, Foster observed, were excellent.

Drab as was the environment of the new capital, the town did not lack for colorful visitors. For instance, on November 30, 1805, an envoy from Tunis, Sidi Soliman Mellimelli (as his name is usually spelled in American documents), arrived with an exotic retinue, including three huge black bodyguards dressed in scarlet. Mellimelli himself was resplendent in scarlet and gold, bright-yellow Moroccan shoes, white silk hose, and twenty yards of white muslin wound into a turban around his head. Mellimelli's mission for a time created a nine days' wonder as small boys haunted his hotel to gain a sight of him and his brilliantly garbed companions.

At the same time, Washington was crowded with American Indian delegations coming to pay their respects to the Great White Father. Mellimelli was fascinated by these visitors and questioned them about their religion, asking them whether they believed in Mohammed, Abraham, or Jesus. When they professed to recognize only the Great Spirit, he pronounced them heretics. Foster noted in his journal that squaws who came with their husbands to the capital observed the deference shown women by white men and shamed their spouses into imitation of these courtesies; the squaws even sat on their horses until their husbands helped them down like other Washington women, a thing hitherto unheard of in Indian society.

Though Washington was a capital in a swamp, it was not devoid of entertainment and amusements. Dinner parties, then as now, were the commonest form of social entertain-

The "city" of Washington—a mere village on the east bank of the Potomac—as it appeared in 1800, when the capital was moved here from the flourishing metropolis of Philadelphia. *Engraving by Heath, 1804, after Parkyns. Courtesy, Library of Congress.*

The White House—or President's House, as it was officially known at the time—did not originally have the north and south porticoes by which we identify it today. This watercolor by the architect Benjamin Latrobe, dated 1807, shows the original east façade with his design for the porticoes, subsequently added. *Courtesy, Library of Congress.*

Vew of the East front of the Presidents House with the addition of the North & South Porticos

ment; the cocktail party had not yet been invented. Men with sporting instincts could always go hunting in the nearby woods. English visitors laughed at Americans for using the term "hunting" for all types of game, including birds, when a proper Englishman always used the term "shooting" for small game, "hunting" being reserved for foxes. Horse races were held at Georgetown. Alexandria had a small theater and a good inn, Gadsby's, which attracted visitors from Washington willing to make so long a journey. Barbecues and picnics in the summer were also diverting, as were elaborate balls and impromptu dances held in the winter. Card games at which men often played for high stakes scandalized some of the more puritanical, as did the large consumption of whiskey by Washington men.

Political feelings sometimes ran high in the capital, and hosts had to choose guests carefully to avoid quarrels at social gatherings. Foster complained that he had great trouble arranging his parties "so as to avoid giving occasion for quarrels, especially as there were several hot-headed Irishmen in Congress who would have desired no better sport than to shoot at [John] Randolph or any other leading member of the opposition."[3]

The tendency to quarrel was not helped by the amount of spiritous liquor consumed. Foster was astonished to discover in his travels through Virginia a drink new to him, something called a mint julep, "compounded of brandy, sugar, mint leaves, and water," which his host told him "the Virginians were in the habit of taking before breakfast."[4] Later bourbon whiskey was substituted for the brandy.

Barbecues, at which a pig, spitted on green hickory sticks, was roasted in an open pit over oak coals, attracted large crowds, even of "the better sort of people," says Foster somewhat snobbishly. Ordinarily held in the woods near a tavern, the barbecue was sometimes followed by a dance and other jollification. To what extent the "better sort" took part in the goings-on that followed the feast

By 1839 the capital was beginning to look more like a town, but a rural one. Chickens, unperturbed by traffic, roam freely. *Anonymous pen-and-ink drawing, 1839. Courtesy, Library of Congress.*

Foster does not indicate. During political campaigns a barbecue was a sure way to get a crowd to listen to opposing candidates, who were expected to speak from the same platform. In this way voters could gain an impression of the candidates' capabilities and make up their minds about their qualifications.

Even in a relatively sophisticated place like Washington foreigners were distressed at what they considered the bad manners of Americans in asking too many personal questions. To English visitors especially this invasion of privacy was annoying. Foster reports the experience of a refugee French general, Jean Victor Moreau, who was so plagued by questioners that he finally found a congenial fishing companion who knew no word of French. Since Moreau knew no English, they got on famously together.

Although the manners of Americans impressed Foster as somewhat effusive, he gave a more favorable picture of them than did many of his countrymen. For example, on a visit to Norfolk he comments on the "frank familiarity of the Norfolk people who shake one another's hands most heartily, men and women, whenever they meet. Even in my case, though a stranger, the hat was never touched to me, but my hand was seized hold of in the street, and again the same cordial salutation was repeated by way of welcome on my entering a gentleman's house."[5] He concluded that in some respects Virginians had better manners than Europeans. For instance, one could leave a group without being pressed to stay, and at meals nobody urged one to eat more than enough, "as sometimes will happen in English country towns."

The commentary of tourists in the new American Republic was usually colored by the visitor's own political views. Liberals favoring the republican form of government endeavored to see the best side of the United States, including the manners of its citizens. Conservatives who regarded republics as hardly better than Communist states found little good to say about the young nation and its people.

One commentator whose work was widely circulated was Mrs. Frances Trollope, author of *Domestic Manners of the Americans*, first published in 1832; she was the mother of Anthony Trollope, the novelist. Mrs. Trollope, a quixotic woman, had come to America in 1827 to try to mend the family fortunes by establishing a department store in Cincinnati. After three years—and a complete failure of her enterprise—she returned to England with a sheaf of notes, a sour stock of recollections, and a determination to see whether she could pay her debts by describing her experiences. She succeeded beyond her expectations, and her book was read with pleasure in England and with annoyance in the United States. Americans maintained that she had slandered them in a scandalous fashion, but Mark Twain later observed that "she was merely telling the truth." At any rate, Americans did not like "the truth" as Mrs. Trollope told it, and they reviled her as "old Dame Trollope" and accused her of malicious lying.

Mrs. Trollope, whose work was used by conservatives as

propaganda against liberal doctrines, ironically was persuaded to go to America by Frances Wright, a wealthy Scottish-born reformer, who had dreams of establishing a society in the wilds of Tennessee where free love and communal sharing of possessions would liberate men from the tyranny of greed. Miss Wright visited the Trollopes in the autumn of 1827 and gave such a favorable picture of backwoods America that Mrs. Trollope, two daughters, and son Henry, aged sixteen (who was not doing well at Winchester College), set sail with Miss Wright late in the same year. Mr. Trollope would follow later.

A visit to Miss Wright's primitive colony at Nashoba, in the woods some fifteen miles beyond Memphis, proved uncomfortable and disillusioning, and Mrs. Trollope moved on to Cincinnati, which she had heard would be the ideal spot for a store selling European goods. Cincinnati was a fast-growing town on the Ohio River, principally noted at the time for its curing of pork and hence called Porkopolis by the irreverent. There at a cost of $24,000 (partially on credit) Mrs. Trollope erected a fantastic structure which she called her Bazaar. It was a turreted and many-roomed affair, Gothic, Egyptian, Grecian, and Moorish, and totally impractical for the purposes intended. Although Mrs. Trollope loaded up on goods from England and France, she did not select items desired by residents of Cincinnati, and buyers were few. She even tried using the Bazaar for dramatic performances, musicals, and recitations, but nothing succeeded. In the end her creditors seized her stock, and she had to return to England, but not before visiting Washington, Baltimore, and Philadelphia, where she carefully made notes with a pen dipped in acid.

In Mrs. Trollope's eyes everything in America was inferior to its counterpart in Europe. Even apples were smaller and wormier. Like many another of her countrymen, she objected to the way Americans spoke the King's English. Certain words used here grated on her ears. She disliked hearing "I reckon" and "I guess." She commented:

69

A view from Georgetown of the new "Federal City" on the Potomac at the time it became the capital of the United States. *Aquatint by T. Cartwright, 1801, after G. Beck. Courtesy, Library of Congress.*

"I very seldom during my whole stay in the country heard a sentence elegantly turned and correctly pronounced from the lips of an American. There is always something either in the expression or the accent that jars the feelings and shocks the taste."[6]

No woman's liberation fanatic could have been more bitter about the manners of American men than Mrs. Trollope. Those she encountered on steamboats on the Mississippi and the Ohio and at inns where she was forced to stay were almost a total offense to her because of their tobacco chewing and spitting, their whiskey drinking, and their habit of eating onions and blowing their onion-tobacco-whiskey breaths her way. "Let no one who wishes to receive agreeable impressions of American manners commence their travels in a Mississippi steamboat; . . . I would infinitely prefer sharing the apartment of a party of well conditioned pigs to being confined to its cabin. I hardly know any annoyance

70

so deeply repugnant to English feelings as the incessant, remorseless spitting of Americans."[7] She constantly complains throughout *Domestic Manners of the Americans* about this habit, as did many other tourists, including Charles Dickens a little later. Tobacco chewing was one of the most repugnant of American habits. Mrs. Trollope in another passage describes social gatherings where the men herd together and leave the women segregated to engage in small talk. "The gentlemen spit, talk of elections and the price of produce, and spit again," she notes.[8] "I am inclined to think this most vile and universal habit of chewing tobacco is the cause of a remarkable peculiarity in the male physiognomy of Americans," she observes after a visit to a session of Congress in Washington; "their lips are almost uniformly thin and compressed." Congressmen did not impress her with their dignity. "The spitting was incessant, and not one in ten of the male part of the illustrious legislative audience sat according to the usual custom of human beings; the legs were thrown sometimes over the front of the box, sometimes over the side of it; here and there a senator stretched his entire length along a bench, and in many instances the front rail was preferred as a seat."[9]

Table manners shocked Mrs. Trollope. At the inns and in dining saloons on steamboats, guests rushed to their meals, gobbled down their food hurriedly and in silence, and showed scant courtesy to anyone. "The total want of all the usual courtesies of the table, the voracious rapidity with which the viands were seized and devoured, the strange uncouth phrases and pronunciation, the loathsome spitting, from the contamination of which it was absolutely impossible to protect our dresses, the frightful manner of feeding with their knives till the whole blade seemed to enter into the mouth, and the still more frightful manner of cleaning the teeth afterwards with a pocket knife soon forced us to feel that . . . the dinner hour was to be anything rather than an hour of enjoyment," she comments after a meal on a Mississippi steamboat.[10]

71

Even the consumption of watermelons, which she grudgingly admitted she learned to eat with some pleasure, annoyed Mrs. Trollope:

> Many wagon-loads of enormous watermelons were brought to market every day, and I was sure to see groups of men, women, and children seated on the pavement round the spot where they were sold, sucking in prodigious quantities of this watery fruit. Their manner of devouring them is extremely unpleasant. The huge fruit is cut into half a dozen sections of about a foot long and then, dripping as it is with water, applied to the mouth, from either side of which pour copious streams of the fluid, while ever and anon, a mouthful of the hard black seeds are shot out in all directions to the great annoyance of all within reach. When I first tasted this fruit I thought it very vile stuff indeed, but before the end of the season we all learned to like it. When taken with claret and sugar it makes delicious wine and water.[11]

Religious revivals and camp meetings horrified Mrs. Trollope, and she described some of the itinerant preachers as deadbeats or worse. Particularly unpleasant, in her opinion, were the hysterical seizures experienced by young girls who fell to the ground in paroxysms of fear at the threats of hell awaiting miserable sinners.

In short, Mrs. Trollope found little to commend in her observation of American conduct. All the talk of "equality" in the American Republic to her was bombast and twaddle, and she took pleasure in reproving Englishmen who were taken in by such American views. "And here again it may be observed," she comments, "that the theory of equality may be daintily discussed by English gentlemen in a London dining room when the servant . . . respectfully shuts the door and leaves them to their walnuts and their wisdom. But it will be found less palatable when it presents itself in the shape of a hard, greasy paw and is claimed in accents that breathe less of freedom than of onions and whiskey. Strong, indeed, must be the love of equality in an English breast if it can survive a tour through the Union."[12] No wonder that reactionaries in England used Mrs. Trollope's book as propaganda against various movements for reform.

Not all visitors to America were so harsh as Mrs. Trollope, but many reports described the ferocity of fights on the frontier when men gouged out an opponent's eyes if possible or slaughtered him with a bowie knife, a sharp-bladed weapon, perhaps invented by Rezin P. Bowie or his brother James. It could be used for skinning, cutting up meat, eating, or stabbing an enemy. Every frontiersman, before the invention of the six-shooter, carried a bowie knife in his belt.

One frontier story told of a visitor to a saloon in San Francisco early in the morning before the proprietor had swept out. "What are all those grapes doing on the floor?" the visitor asked. "Them ain't grapes," the saloonkeeper replied. "We had right much fighting here last night and them are eyeballs that got gouged out."

But Americans did not need critics like Mrs. Trollope and a host of others from her country to tell them of their shortcomings and to urge them to mend their manners. A numerous body of American writers set about improving American behavior by publishing books on conduct and etiquette, a type of work that has continued to attract readers to the present day. In a little volume entitled *Learning How to Behave: A Historical Study of American Etiquette Books*, Arthur M. Schlesinger, Sr., describes the efforts of these reformers.

Some of the American writers insisted that they did not recommend the artificial drawing-room manners of the effete Old World, the fops, dandies, and fine ladies of European courts, but they wanted Americans to develop a natural courtesy, a thoughtfulness of others, and a politeness consistent with republican ideals. Newspapers and maga-

73

zines ran sections on manners and morals, which they managed to equate.

Guidance in good manners had a prominent place in a popular periodical, *Godey's Lady's Book*. Catharine M. Sedgwick was the author of *Morals of Manners* (New York, 1846), in which she endeavored, sometimes by satire, to instill a sense of courtesy in her readers and to shame them from habits of rudeness. So popular did etiquette books become in the 1850's that the publisher of dime novels Irwin P. Beadle brought out the *Dime Book of Practical Etiquette* (New York, 1859), a work that made guidance in manners available to anyone who could afford ten cents.

The advice in many of these books was often terse and explicit. Even if a gentleman bathes only twice a year, he ought to change his linen every day, one book advised. Another warned that a gentleman should not sit in the house with his hat on in the presence of ladies. Spitting, which so worried Mrs. Trollope, came under the ban of the etiquette books, as did bad table manners.

If Americans did not improve in manners, as well as in morals, it was not for lack of handbooks to tell them what to do and, more important, what not to do. Guides were plentiful, and readers avidly bought them. A zeal for self-improvement was one of the characteristics of Americans in the nineteenth century. If they did not choose to imitate the manners of Englishmen, they at least sought to establish a code of good manners of their own. Silk purses could not be made out of every sow's ear, nor could every lout be transformed into a gentleman, but countless authors turned their attention to the task. The results were evident in the improved behavior of Americans as time wore on and the Republic developed in maturity.

Chapter 5

The Excitement
and Trials of Travel

From early in the history of the settlement of North America its people have been restless and much given to moving and to travel. The English diplomat in the United States in Jefferson's administration, Augustus John Foster, commented on this quality of Americans. On a trip through Virginia he spent the night at a settlement on the Rapidan River. His host, a Scot about fifty years old, had a fine farm, an excellent orchard, and a good house, but he was talking about moving west to Tennessee or Mississippi, because, Foster points out, "the struggle to be comfortable and rich has more charms for these transatlantic settlers than the actual attainment of their object."[1] This quality of restless movement, of a desire to try living in some other place, of curiosity about other regions, has accounted for a shifting of populations, as well as travel for pleasure and excitement, throughout our history.

Travel even between nearby cities was an adventure in the early days when roads were often merely muddy tracks or dusty trails with sparse accommodations along the way. Vehicles and conveyances consisted of lumbering coaches with inadequate springs, carts, or heavy wagons. Even women often found horseback riding preferable to coaches. The numerous rivers provided the smoothest means of transportation in sailboats, canoes, or bateaux, soon to be superseded by steamboats. Coastal vessels carried passengers and freight between towns accessible by sea. By the 1830's railways were being built, and steam cars in the first half of the nineteenth century could be both exciting and hazardous.

Whatever the hazards, inconveniences, and discomfort, Americans, old and young, were eager to travel. Distant pastures always looked greener, distant land always beckoned, and if Americans had no other reason for moving about, they traveled because of curiosity about other localities and for sheer adventure. They had not yet become addicted to either speed or comfort. Plodding along on foot at three miles an hour or jogging on a horse at only a little faster rate, they were content to spend the better part of a day reaching a nearby town. In regions without inns or taverns travelers were accustomed to ask overnight accommodations at any house they reached by nightfall. In some places a lonely householder was so glad to see a visitor that he welcomed the stranger and refused payment for the night's lodging and breakfast; others, however, were glad to take pay. Sometimes the traveler, overtaken by night in a poor region, had to sleep on the floor, wrapped in his overcoat or blanket that he carried; occasionally he was asked to sleep in the loft on a straw tick with the children of the household. Many a traveler accustomed to better things was glad for any kind of shelter. Where there were inns and taverns, they were often dirty and vermin-ridden. Yet none of these handicaps discouraged travelers from taking the open road.

Before the War of Independence the thirteen colonies were ill served with highways, and if a traveler had wanted to go overland from Maine to Georgia, he would have found nothing to compare with U.S. 1 or any other continuous road, for none existed.

76

There were but a few good hostelries along major highways that became regular stagecoach stops. Such was the fieldstone inn pictured here in a painting of Lancaster Pike, Pennsylvania, in winter, 1795. *Artist unknown. Courtesy, U.S. Bureau of Public Roads.*

George Washington, when commander of American troops during the war, ordered maps to be made of such roads as existed in the principal areas of military operations. In 1789 Christopher Colles published the first of a series of maps which he brought out in the next few years with the general title of *A Survey of the Roads of the United States of America*; this series provided maps for the chief roads between Albany, New York, and Yorktown, Virginia. Colles' work (reprinted with an explanatory introduction in 1961 by the Harvard University Press) represented the first systematic attempt to provide travelers with a road book of the nation.

The most striking characteristic of these maps for the modern reader is the scarcity of roads. An adventurer trying to get from Albany to Yorktown would have to make a circuitous trip, and even then he would find long gaps where no road was marked. His best course would be to go by road to some port, take a coastal vessel to another port in the general direction that he was traveling, and then try to find a road from that point to another port where he could pick up a boat for part of the journey. Many travelers did make north-south journeys in this fashion, mixing road and water routes so as to cut down their mileage as best they could.

In an age of air travel it is difficult to remember the

slowness of transport early in the nation's history. About the time Colles was publishing his maps, new roads were being marked out through the forests, often merely by cutting down trees and leaving the stumps through which a wheeled vehicle had to make its way. One traveler, commenting on such a road, declared that the muddy ruts between the stumps were so deep that he scarcely made more than thirteen miles in four hours.

Before the Revolution a stagecoach journey between New York and Philadelphia required from two to three days, though in 1771 newspapers announced a coach with phenomenal speed, Mercereau's Flying Machine stage, which could make the journey in a day and a half.

Soon after the Revolution regular stage lines began operating between Richmond, Virginia, and New York and from Boston to New York. Depending on the weather and the state of the roads, a coach traveler could count on making from twenty-five to sixty miles in a day. The normal stint for a coach was about twenty miles between taverns, where passengers transferred to another coach with fresh horses.

Colles' maps give symbols indicating taverns, blacksmith shops, churches, and jails. The blacksmith shop was almost as important as a modern filling station, for horses were constantly casting a shoe and needing to be reshod; coaches frequently broke a wheel or an axle and had to be repaired while the passengers waited.

When President Washington made the trip from Alexandria, Virginia, to New York for his inauguration in 1789, it took from April 17 to April 23, seven days by coach, varied at intervals when the President mounted a horse for a ceremonial ride through some town. Washington made the journey as rapidly as possible, though he was hindered by formal dinners and addresses of welcome along the way; despite these ceremonies, he was usually on the way by sunrise and did not stop until nightfall.

Road building was fairly rapid in the early years of the

78

nineteenth century, especially in the more thickly populated sections of the country. Elias Boudinot, a prosperous citizen of Burlington, New Jersey, set out from home in June, 1809, in his private carriage, bound for Boston. He kept a journal in which he constantly notes the fine state of the "excellent turnpikes." Even in the more sparsely settled South, roads were improving, and travel became less fatiguing and dangerous. To facilitate travel to the West, the federal government built what was known as the National Road, which led from Baltimore to Cumberland, Maryland, and thence to Wheeling, West Virginia. By 1833 it had been extended to Columbus, Ohio. Portions of the road were paved with flat stones, and some not so flat, which caused complaints from travelers jolting over it in wheeled vehicles. An older trail called the Wilderness Road had been used by emigrants to Kentucky since shortly before the Revolution. This road started from a point on the Holston River in Tennessee, crossed the mountains through the Cumberland Gap, and continued on to Harrodsburg, Kentucky. Once across the mountains, travelers sought rivers flowing into the Ohio and thence down the Mississippi. Journeys on waterways were much easier than land travel.

Before the days of steamboats navigable rivers were filled with a variety of craft ranging from birchbark canoes to huge flatboats and rafts. Boatmen on the Ohio built large roofed barges called Kentucky arks. An emigrating family headed farther west could load their household goods, hay, grain, and livestock on one of these arks and float down the Ohio and the Mississippi to the desired destination. Keelboats, as the name suggests, were flatboats built with a keel to give them added strength. They were usually decked at each end with a planked runway along each side. Crewmen with long poles could walk along this runway to propel the keelboats in shallow water. They were also equipped with oars and occasionally a sail. When Lewis and Clark set out on their famous exploring expedition, they used a keelboat

79

An emigrant family floating down the Mississippi on a flat-boat. Note the poultry peering out of their cage under the fiddler and hams hanging in the bow. *Currier and Ives lithograph, 1870. Courtesy, Library of Congress.*

to convey the bulk of their supplies up the Missouri River. Barges, flatboats, and arks were cheap and easy to build; they could be used to float goods and passengers to down-river towns, St. Louis and New Orleans. There an emigrating family could sell the craft for lumber and proceed to whatever point in the West they had selected.

Travel on these rivercraft was dangerous. Both the Ohio and the Mississippi were infested by thugs and lawless types of all sorts. River pirates sometimes seized loaded rafts and flatboats and threw the owners and passengers overboard. Hostile Indians were also a threat, for their arrows and gunfire from the wooded banks along narrow reaches of the rivers could be disastrous. The weather could be tricky, and sudden squalls could upset a boat or drive it onto a sandbar. The streams were filled with fallen trees and snags which had to be avoided. In short, navigating any craft on the great rivers required both courage and skill. Even so, such travel was preferable to journeys on land along wilderness ways.

A revolution in water travel came with the invention of the steamboat. James Rumsey, a Maryland inventor and promoter, in 1787 launched a successful steamboat on the Potomac River that moved at the exciting speed of four miles an hour. Although Rumsey obtained a charter to operate steamboats in Maryland, Virginia, and New York, nothing came of his project. Four years later John Fitch, another inventor and promoter, launched a steamboat on the Delaware River that attained twice the speed of Rumsey's craft. But it remained for Robert Fulton to operate the first steamboat that was commercially successful. In 1807 his famous *Clermont* made the trip on the Hudson River from New York to Albany, a distance of 150 miles, in thirty-two hours. Within the next twenty years steamboats became a common means of travel on most of the navigable rivers of the country. They were cheaply built of wood; using simple engines, they were propelled by means of a stern wheel or side wheels, and they used for fuel wood obtained from woodpiles along the shore. All these river steamboats rode high in the water, usually with three towering decks and a couple of tall smokestacks belching smoke and sparks. Fires were frequent, and boiler explosions wrecked many vessels with appalling loss of life.

These dangers did not deter travelers who enjoyed the

Robert Fulton's steamboat *Clermont* on its maiden voyage on the Hudson River, New York to Albany, 1807. *Etching by S. Hollyer, 1907. Courtesy, Library of Congress.*

Of the many steamboat explosions and fires, one of the
most spectacular was the "awful conflagration of the Steam
Boat *Lexington* in Long Island Sound on Monday Evening,
January 13th, 1840, by which melancholy occurrence over
100 persons perished." *Lithograph by N. Currier after W. K.
Hewitt. Courtesy, Library of Congress.*

excitement of a race between riverboats, even when fool-
hardy captains ordered the firemen to stoke the boilers with
pine knots and sometimes even with sides of fat bacon to
produce the maximum steam and consequent speed. Rival-
ries between pilots were keen. A roving reporter named
Edmund Flagg described a race on the Mississippi in the
summer of 1837. As the steamboat in which he was traveling up the Mississippi emerged from a particularly dangerous portion of the river, her pilot observed another craft
nearby, "and then," says Flagg, "commenced one of those
perilous feats of rivalry frequent upon western waters, A
Race. Directly before us, a steamer of a large class, deeply
laden, was roaring and struggling against the torrent under
her highest pressure. During our passage we had several
times passed and repassed each other . . . but now as evening came on, and we found ourselves gaining upon our
antagonist, the excitement of emulation flushed every
cheek. The passengers and crew hung clustering in breath-
less interest upon the galleries and the boiler deck, . . .
[they watched as the engineer] glided like a spectre among

the fearful elements of destruction [and] gave evidence that the challenge was accepted."

Because of fog the steamers had to tie up for the night, but the next morning the race was resumed, and the rival vessel, in overtaking Flagg's steamer, "attempted, contrary to all rules and regulations . . . , to pass between our boat and the bank beneath which we were moving, an outrage which . . . would have sent us to the bottom." Some of the passengers got out their guns and were prepared to open fire on the onrushing vessel when it reversed its engines. "The sole cause for this outrage . . . was a private pique existing between the pilots of the respective steamers," Flagg concluded.[2] Not every boat race ended without disaster, for sometimes the boilers burst, hurling the passengers into the stream.

Of all the rivers, the Missouri was perhaps the most dangerous for steamboat travelers. George Catlin, the painter of Indian life, who made a journey up the Missouri in 1832, described the difficulties of navigation:

I arrived at the mouth of the Yellowstone [River], Upper Missouri, yesterday, in the steamer *Yellow Stone* after a voyage of nearly three months from St. Louis, a distance of two thousand miles, the greater part of which has never before been navigated by steam. . . . For the distance of 1,000 miles above St. Louis, the shores of this river (and in many places, the whole bed of the stream) are filled with snags and raft, formed of trees of the largest size, which have been undermined by the falling banks and cast into the stream; their roots becoming fastened in the bottom of the river, with their tops floating on the surfaces of the water and pointing down the stream, forming the most frightful and discouraging prospect for the adventurous voyageur. Almost every island and sand-bar is covered with huge piles of these floating trees, and when the river is flooded, its surface is almost literally covered with floating raft and driftwood which bid positive defiance to keel-boats and steamers on their way up the river.[3]

Catlin, like Lewis and Clark before him, was struck by the muddiness of the Missouri and the constant caving in of its banks. As the rich earth fell into the boiling current, the water took on the color of coffee or chocolate, so dark that Catlin could not see a silver coin that he dropped in a tumbler of this polluted water. Yet some of the trappers who used the river maintained that drinking from the Missouri was good for one's health!

Later Mark Twain, in *Life on the Mississippi* (1883), gave a vivid picture of the dangers of snags, sawyers (as floating trees were called), and sandbars in the ever-changing channels of the Mississippi.

Passengers and crews on the river steamers were sometimes boisterous and unruly. Gamblers were frequent among the travelers, and card sharks often managed to separate gullible passengers from their money. Mrs. Frances Trollope, who made a voyage from New Orleans to Memphis in January, 1828, on board the *Belvedere*, was not pleased with either her accommodations or her fellow travelers. "We had a full complement of passengers on board," she remarked.

The deck, as is usual, was occupied by the Kentucky flatboat men returning from New Orleans after having disposed of the boat and cargo which they had conveyed thither, with no more labor than that of steering her, the current bringing her down at the rate of four miles an hour. We had about two hundred of these men on board, but the part of the vessel occupied by them is so distinct from the cabins that we never saw them except when we stopped to take on wood. And then they ran, or rather sprung and vaulted over each other's heads, to the shore whence

84

they all assisted in carrying wood to supply the steam engine, the performance of this duty being a stipulated part of the payment of their passage.[4]

Mrs. Trollope's manservant, who was quartered among the Kentuckians, reported that they were constantly gambling, quarreling, and engaging in petty thievery. The "gentlemen" whom she met in the dining saloon would not have borne that designation in Europe, she declared, and she was disgusted at their crudity. They also terrified her with tall tales of the horrors of the river, including crocodiles which devoured whole families. Mrs. Trollope believed these outrageous yarns and jotted them down in her notebook as evidence of the dreadful state of frontier America. She was not comforted when the *Belvedere* ran aground on a sandbar and was stuck there two days before it could reach Memphis in the dead of night during a tempestuous rainstorm.

Another form of water travel, much used by Americans in the first half of the nineteenth century, was by canalboat on the numerous artificial waterways built to improve transportation in the days before railways superseded them. By the 1840's the country was bisected with numerous canals linking navigable rivers and lakes; the primary purpose of the canals was the carriage of freight, but canalboats also accepted passengers who had the leisure to endure a slow but smooth form of transport.

The dream of linking the East with the West by means of waterways had long interested American promoters. At the conclusion of the War of Independence General Washington concerned himself with a project to discover a water route from the Potomac to the Ohio and Mississippi rivers. On September 1, 1784, with three companions (including his nephew Bushrod Washington) and three servants, Washington set out on a horseback journey to the West to inspect lands he owned on the Ohio and to investigate a possible water route. The trip took him to Miller's Run, southwest of Pittsburgh, over Braddock's Road and past spots where he had soldiered in his youth, and convinced him that a water route by way of the North Branch of the Potomac was feasible. On this journey he met James Rumsey, who demonstrated a small-scale model of his steamboat, and was much impressed by him. The trip was arduous and indicates the hardships of overland travel at this time. At one spot the party had to sleep in the forest with no other covering from the rain but their overcoats.

Washington exerted his energies to promote the development of navigation between the Potomac and the Ohio and in 1785 became president of the Potomac Company. The Virginia Assembly in gratitude presented him with twenty-five shares of stock in the company, which he accepted with the understanding that he would devote the stock to some philanthropic use. He later bequeathed the stock to help found a national university in Washington. The Potomac Company proposed to build a canal around the Great Falls of the Potomac above Georgetown and to make the North Branch of the Potomac navigable as far as possible. From the Potomac freight would be carried by wagons over a portage to the Cheat River and thence by the Monongahela to the Ohio.

The Potomac Company did not succeed, but the plan survived; in 1828 the Chesapeake and Ohio Canal was begun, and by 1850 it was completed as far as Cumberland, Maryland. Its planners hoped to reach a tributary of the Ohio by means of a tunnel through the mountains, but that failed. The Chesapeake and Ohio Canal came too late, for by the time of its completion the Baltimore and Ohio Railway, which paralleled it, made it obsolete.

The most successful canal was the Erie, which connected the Hudson River and Lake Erie. As early as 1788 such a canal was proposed, but not until 1825 was it completed. On October 25 of that year the canalboat *Seneca Chief* set out from Buffalo to make the first trip from the Great Lakes to New York City. It arrived on November 4, bearing from

A view of the Erie Canal at Lockport, Niagara County, New York. Several of the ten locks at this point are visible (right center), the gradation in water level clearly marked by the descending order of water gates, or locks. Note the canalboat being pulled by a mule team on the towpath at far right. *Lithograph by Bufford, 1836, after W. Wilson. Courtesy, Library of Congress.*

Lake Erie a barrel of water, which was ceremoniously emptied into the Atlantic. The Erie Canal, an enormous success, made New York a prosperous market for products of the West. Soon feeder canals were being built, and towns were growing along its route from Albany to Buffalo. The success of the Erie promoted canal developments throughout the country, to be stopped only by the building of railroads.

An anonymous account of a journey on the Erie Canal, published in a Philadelphia magazine in 1829, gives an idea of this type of travel. The writer chose to go by stagecoach from Albany to Schenectady because of the tediousness of that portion of the journey, since the canalboat had to pass through forty locks in twenty-eight miles and took twenty-four hours to make the passage. But at Schenectady he bargained for a passage with wildly competing ticket sellers and went aboard a vessel of the Clinton Line. The fare was computed at the rate of a cent-and-a-quarter per mile.

The boat, with berths for thirty persons forward and a dining room aft, was primarily for cargo stowed in the center section. "The roof," the writer explained, "is in the form of the back of a tortoise and affords a handsome promenade excepting when the everlasting bridges and locks open their mouths for your heads."[5]

The numerous bridges over the canal were a constant danger, for sometimes there was only a foot of clearance between the top of the boat and the bridge. As a warning the captain would sing out "low bridge," but his call did not always come in time to save a luckless passenger on the "promenade." "The Captain informed me that six persons have lost their lives by being crushed between the bridges, which is a greater number than have been killed during the same time by the bursting of steam engines in the waters of the middle and eastern states," this writer noted lugubriously.

Canalboats were hauled by two or three horses or mules driven along the towpath. The tow rope, sometimes thirty yards long, was ordinarily attached to a timber amidships. The rate of speed varied from three to four miles an hour, depending on the weight of the cargo. A fresh team was hooked on every twenty miles.

Most canalboats served food, though on some of the cheaper cargo craft passengers had to provide their own rations. A few boats on the Erie Canal were deluxe vessels that carried only passengers and boasted luxurious quarters, good food and drink, and fine table silver. They assured customers that they could glide to Buffalo at a speed of four miles an hour and would have priority at the locks. Canal travelers in the nineteenth century must have been possessed of phenomenal patience.

The Best Friend of Charleston, with its trolleylike cars, was built in New York City and sent by steamship to Charleston, where it arrived on October 23, 1830. After several trials, it made its first excursion trip, pictured here, on January 15, 1831. *Wood engraving in William H. Brown's* History of the First Locomotives in America, *1877. Courtesy, Library of Congress.*

At the height of enthusiasm for canals, advocates of railroads came to disturb the canal builders' dreams of prosperity. In a relatively short time railroads became a mania with Americans, and they remained a romantic symbol of progress throughout the nineteenth century. Indeed, only in our time have railroads lost their appeal. In an earlier day most small boys could dream of no more appealing career than that of a locomotive engineer, and the hoarse whistle of an oncoming engine was enough to send children—and even adults—scurrying to see the passing train.

The first locomotive to pull a string of cars on a railway track in the United States was called the Best Friend of Charleston and performed its feat in December, 1830, on six miles of track of the Charleston and Hamburg line, being built to connect Charleston, South Carolina, with the head of navigation on the Savannah River at what is now Augusta, Georgia. The village on the South Carolina side was called Hamburg.

The Best Friend attained a speed of 30 miles an hour without cars attached and with four loaded cars could make from 16 to 21 miles per hour. This foretold a favorable speed that would far exceed anything the canals could hope to offer. The American love of speed was beginning. By 1833 the line was completed all the way to Hamburg, a distance of 136 miles, which at the time made it the world's longest railroad.

Unhappily the Best Friend's boilers blew up in 1831, a calamity that caused great concern to the promoters of the railway until Horatio Allen, the superintendent, conceived the notion of a barrier car with a wall of cotton bales between the locomotive and the passengers. Travelers behind the next locomotive, the West Point, felt reassured in case its boilers exploded.

Although the Charleston and Hamburg line was the first to operate successfully with steam, it was not the first to be chartered. In 1827 a group of Baltimore businessmen, fearful that the Erie Canal was going to drain away too much business from their town, obtained a charter for the Baltimore and Ohio Railroad. On July 4, 1828, Charles Carroll, last surviving signer of the Declaration of Independence, turned the first spadeful of dirt to mark the beginning of construction of the B & O. By May, 1830, its wooden rails had reached Ellicott Mills, a distance of some fourteen miles, and the directors declared the road open for business —at least that far. But the B & O used horses to pull its cars, and it even experimented with sail-cars. In the meantime Peter Cooper had built a locomotive of his own design, the Tom Thumb, which he demonstrated with such success that he persuaded the officers of the B & O to switch to steam. By 1842 the line stretched all the way to Cumberland, and by 1857, by using connecting lines, passengers on the B & O could get to St. Louis by rail.

By 1835 everybody was talking about railroads, and every town was hoping to promote one. A Frenchman, Michael Chevalier, was sent by his government to this country in 1833 to study American canals and railroads, the fame of which had already reached Europe. He stayed for two years and wrote a fascinating series of letters describing the country and his reactions to it. He was particularly impressed by everybody's excitement over railroads. "The benefits of the invention are so palpable to their prac-

"Exciting trial of speed between Mr. Peter Cooper's Locomotive, 'Tom Thumb' and one of Stockton and Stokes' Horse-cars." The race on the Baltimore and Ohio Railroad, held on August 28, 1830, was instrumental in changing over the B & O from horse-power to steam. *Engraving in Brown,* History of the First Locomotive, *1871. Courtesy, Eleutherian Mills Historical Library.*

tical good sense," he asserted, "that they endeavor to make an application of it everywhere and to everything, rightly or wrongly. When they cannot construct a real, profitable railroad across the country from river to river, from city to city, or from state to state, they get one up, at least as a plaything or until they can accomplish something better, under the form of a machine."[6]

Chevalier listed a number of railroads already constructed or a-building. "From New York to Philadelphia, there will soon be not only one open to travel but two. . . . The passage between the two cities will be made in seven hours, five hours on the railroad, and two in the steamboat. . . . From Philadelphia travelers go to Baltimore by the Delaware and Chesapeake, and the Newcastle and Frenchtown railroad in eight hours; from Baltimore to Washington, a railroad has been resolved upon, a company chartered, the shares taken, and the work begun, all within the space of a few months." Other railroads excited his interest, and he predicted that soon one could go from New York to New Orleans by rail.

Some of the railroads tried to solve the problem of getting over the Allegheny Mountains by building inclined planes and hauling the cars up to the next level with cables powered by stationary engines. Of these Chevalier comments that they were "originally designed only for the transportation of goods, but passenger cars have been set up on them at the risk of breaking the necks of travelers."[7] Whatever the risk, travelers were eager to try the new steam cars.

One of the most important rail links with the West was the New York and Erie, completed in 1851 across the southern tier of New York counties to Lake Erie. To celebrate the event, a great gathering of notables assembled on May 14, 1851, to make the journey over the new line. The company included the President of the United States, Millard Fillmore, his Secretary of State, the aged Daniel Webster, and nearly 300 other important figures in business and politics. The party traveled on two special trains. Daniel Webster insisted on riding in a rocking chair lashed to a flatcar so that he would not miss any of the scenery. Along part of the road Webster's train raced along at nearly a mile a minute, a speed that must have tested the old statesman's courage as he held onto his stovepipe hat and battled the cinders raining upon him.

The trains made an overnight stop at Elmira, where the crowd demanded and received a speech from Webster, long known for his oratory. The next day the entourage reached the terminus on the lake at Dunkirk, where the celebration was brought to a climax with an immense barbecue and a parade. The table, 300 feet long, was loaded down with barbecued pigs and oxen and every other viand that the planners could think of. The loaves of bread themselves were 10 feet long and 2 feet thick. With food, drink, and oratory, the crowd glorified another transportation link between East and West.

The multiplication of railroads stimulated further travel. Riding the steam cars became an adventure and a sport for young and old. People with business found the trains a new and speedy means of getting where they needed to go. People with leisure boarded the trains for the pleasure of riding at the dizzying speed of forty to fifty miles an hour. It made little difference that they were black with cinders, smoke, and dust at the end of the journey. They had enjoyed one of the great new inventions. It was a far cry from the days when one jolted over rutted roads in a springless coach or slid along a canal at four miles an hour.

Paved or unpaved, roads were full of stones that made the going rough and hazardous to wheels and axles. This accident occurred at Thornville, Ohio, seen "thro' an opening of the primitive forest." *Aquatint by W. J. Bennett, 1841, after George Harvey. Courtesy of Library of Congress.*

Chapter 6

"Getting Ahead":
The Dream of Prosperity

One of the qualities of Americans that impressed foreigners was their ambition to get ahead in the world, to rise in the social scale, and to acquire the material assets to support the status to which they aspired. Some visitors applauded this ambition; others satirized Americans for their greed and their single-minded pursuit of the almighty dollar. Ironically, some of the foreign critics, then as now, who belabored Americans for materialism, had come to this country in search of money.

Such was the case of Mrs. Frances Trollope, who had dreamed of recouping her family fortunes by selling luxury goods to the inhabitants of Cincinnati. When her startling Bazaar turned out to be a failure and her creditors seized the stock which she had not yet paid for, she returned to England to write the *Domestic Manners of the Americans* (1832), an acid commentary.

"During nearly two years that I resided in Cincinnati or its neighborhood," Mrs. Trollope reported, "I neither saw a beggar nor a man of sufficient fortune to permit his ceasing his efforts to increase it; thus every bee in the hive is actively employed in search of that honey of Hybla, vulgarly called money; neither art, science, learning, nor pleasure can seduce them from its pursuit."[1] In another passage she remarked that "nothing can exceed their [the Americans'] activity and perseverance in all kinds of speculation, handicraft, and enterprise which promises a profitable pecuniary result. I heard an Englishman who had been long resident in America declare that . . . he had never overheard Americans conversing without the word DOLLAR being pronounced between them. Such unity of purpose, such sympathy of feeling, can, I believe, be found nowhere else except perhaps in an ants' nest."[2]

To show the Americans' unremitting zeal to get ahead, Mrs. Trollope cited instances that had come to her notice. One neighbor in Cincinnati had particularly interested her, for when she first encountered him, he and his wife and four children were living in one room, and though they had "plenty of beef-steaks and onions for breakfast, dinner, and supper," they had few other comforts. He could neither read nor write, but he plied his trade of woodcutter and rail-splitter with skill, made shrewd bargains that earned him money, built himself a comfortable house and rented out half of it, got a contract for building a bridge at considerable profit, and at length made himself proprietor of a small hotel and grocery store. "I have no doubt that every sun that sets sees him a richer man than when it rose," Mrs. Trollope commented. "He hopes to make his son a lawyer, and I have little doubt that he will live to see him sit in Congress, and when this time arrives, the woodcutter's son will rank with any other member of Congress, not of courtesy but of right, and the idea that his origin is a disadvantage will never occur to the imagination of the most exalted of his fellow-citizens."[3] Mrs. Trollope grudgingly admitted that this sense of equality was "a spur to exertion," but she grumbled that it also led to "coarse familiarity untempered by any shadow of respect." She never got used to the easy informality of Americans who saw no reason to treat this Englishwoman any differently from others.

Most of the settlers who first came to the American colonies hoped to better their conditions, and they looked upon the New World as a land of opportunity, as indeed it was. It so remained for millions of immigrants throughout the nineteenth century. The belief was widespread that anyone by diligence, sobriety, and thrift could acquire a competence and economic independence.

This doctrine was promoted by Benjamin Franklin's maxims in *Poor Richard's Almanac*. The proverbs that Franklin published became a part of the American gospel of success. In 1757 Franklin compiled the best of his proverbs for publication in the *Almanac* for 1758. This compilation, called "The Speech of Father Abraham," was later published in literally hundreds of editions with the significant title of *The Way to Wealth*. There Americans could read the maxims leading to success: "Early to bed and early to rise makes a man healthy, wealthy, and wise. . . . Industry need not wish. . . . At the working man's house, Hunger looks in but dares not enter. . . . God gives all things to Industry; then plough deep while sluggards sleep. . . . Sloth, like rust, consumes faster than labor wears; while the used key is always bright. . . . The sleeping fox catches no poultry. . . . Keep thy shop and thy shop will keep thee. . . . A ploughman on his legs is higher than a gentleman on his knees. . . . 'Tis hard for an empty meal bag to stand upright." These sayings were part of a little narrative in which the wise old man, Father Abraham, advised youth on the way to behave in order to prosper. He concluded with a bit of spiritual counsel in which he warned that "this doctrine, my friend, is Reason and Wisdom; but after all, do not depend too much upon your own Industry, Frugality, and Prudence, though excellent things, for they all may be blasted without the blessing of Heaven; and therefore ask that blessing humbly, and be not uncharitable to those that at present seem to want it, but comfort them. Remember, Job suffered and was afterward prosperous."

Franklin's tract was published many times, not only in America but in many foreign countries, and had an enormous influence for the next century and a half. In fact, its proverbs are still quoted, and it remains in print. Throughout the nineteenth century it was constantly reproduced, imitated, and sometimes plagiarized by other advocates of self-help as a means of achieving material success. In 1850 Freeman Hunt, editor of the *Merchants Magazine*, published his own imitation of Franklin with copious borrowings as *Worth and Wealth: A Collection of Maxims, Morals, and Miscellanies for Merchants and Men of Business*.

Later in the nineteenth century appeared the most complete summary of the doctrine of success that had influenced the previous decades, a huge book compiled by T. L. Haines with the title (borrowed from Freeman Hunt) of *Worth and Wealth. Or the Art of Getting, Saving, and Using Money* (Chicago, 1883). Although this book was published in the second half of the century, it epitomized doctrines that had influenced American ideas of success since Franklin's time. In fact, it borrowed whole chunks of Franklin's *Way to Wealth*. Haines, however, lacked Franklin's sense of humor and Franklin's concept of values other than mere material success. For example, Haines solemnly canonizes the man who succeeds: "The saint of the nineteenth century is the good merchant; he is wisdom for the foolish, strength for the weak, warning to the wicked, and a blessing to all. Build him a shrine in bank and church, in the market and the exchange, or build it not; no saint stands higher than this saint of trade."[4] To reach this blissful state, Haines had a recipe: "Never be idle. If your hands cannot be usefully employed, attend to the cultivation of your mind." Besides thrift and diligence, this manual of success devoted chapters to courtesy, accuracy, prudence, patience, self-dependence, courage, integrity, and other virtues that would ensure prosperity. To encourage young men to follow its advice, the book included a special section entitled

"Testimony of Millionaires," which cited examples of men who had risen from obscurity to great wealth and power, for the most part in the first half of the nineteenth century, by the application of the recommended virtues.

Among the millionaires described was Stephen Girard of Philadelphia, who started in business during the War of Independence as a bottler of cider and claret, acquired a few sloops and a schooner or two, and soon was on his way to prosperity. A somewhat dubious thrust to his rise came from an unexpected source mentioned by Haines: "In 1779 he returned to Philadelphia and entered upon the New Orleans and St. Domingo trade. Shortly after this his prospects were materially aided by the acquisition of fifty thousand dollars deposited in one of his vessels during the insurrection at St. Domingo, and for which the owners never called." Not every thrifty young man could hope for this kind of heaven-sent impetus, but Girard made the most of it, and Haines added succinctly: "He died in 1832, estimated to be worth twelve million dollars." Haines mentioned with approval Girard's efforts to collect a one-cent debt and quoted the millionaire's "fundamental maxim": "Take care of the cents, and the dollars will take care of themselves."[5]

Another millionaire cited by Haines as an example of a man who rose by his own efforts to great wealth was John McDonough, who died in New Orleans in 1850 after acquiring millions in merchandising and real estate. Even before the acquisition of the Louisiana Territory by the United States, McDonough was in New Orleans engaged in deals with the Spanish governor. According to Haines, McDonough early realized the value of "influence" in getting ahead and diligently cultivated the friendship of people in power. When he died, he had some of his maxims for success carved on his tombstone so that boys visiting the graveyard could learn and profit by them. Among these maxims leading to success, Haines quoted McDonough's "Third Rule": "You must pray to the Almighty with fervor and

99

zeal. I never prayed sincerely to God in all my life without having my prayer answered satisfactorily. Follow my advice and you will become a rich man." Haines added his own observations on the value of prayer to the success seeker:

> Prayer prepares the mind for great undertakings; it gives an earnestness and seriousness to the character; it curbs that levity and frivolity which trifle with important concerns, viewing everything as a game; it gives a restraining power in the hour of temptation and makes simple faith mightier than wisdom; it creates a subdued enthusiasm, a calm confidence in eventual success that no present danger can overthrow. . . . God will hear and answer sincere prayer.[6]

The belief that it is virtually a religious duty to struggle for material success was widespread in the first half of the nineteenth century, as it was later. Young men and women received dire warnings against idleness and the waste of God's precious time. This had been a part of seventeenth-century Puritan doctrine and carried over into later American life. A corollary to this doctrine was that God would reward the sober, diligent, and virtuous youth.

Men took pride in being "self-made," and to rise from humble circumstances to affluence and power was an indication of special merit. Some men liked to boast of their struggles to reach the eminence they attained, and their bragging was a source of annoyance to others, especially to foreign visitors, who frequently noted this characteristic in Americans they casually encountered. Insofar as Americans developed a social class, the rich became the aristocrats in the new dispensation. Fisher Ames, a leader among the New England Federalists, declared that society ought to be controlled by the "wise, the good, and the rich."

Not every American, of course, worshiped riches and the rich, but the attitude was widespread. Alexis de Tocqueville, French writer on political theory, arrived in New

York in May, 1831, for a long tour of America. In his *Democracy in America*, first published in France in 1835, he commented that "I know no other country where love of money has such a grip on men's hearts, or where stronger scorn is expressed for the permanent equality of property. But wealth circulates there with incredible rapidity and experience shows that two successive generations seldom enjoy its favors."[7] He later explained the willingness of Americans to take risks which sometimes resulted in the loss of money they had avidly sought: "In the United States fortunes are easily lost and gained again. The country is limitless and full of inexhaustible resources. The people have all the needs and all the appetites of a growing creature who believes that however hard he tries, he will always be surrounded by more good things than he can grasp. . . . Boldness in industrial undertakings is the chief cause of their rapid progress, power, and greatness."[8] For Americans in the early days of the nation, as with their descendants, the pursuit of wealth was a sort of serious sport. If they took the risk and lost, they were confident that their next effort would be more successful. That is not to say that they were careless gamblers with their investments, for business was a matter of grave importance, but they were invariably optimistic. The country had a bright future, and they were sure that they would share in its prosperity.

Although some foreign observers in their commentary gave the impression that Americans were money-mad, the effort to make money represented a profound desire to achieve economic independence. Nineteenth-century Americans knew nothing about government subsidies, and even state aid for the poor—"welfare"—had not yet become a social concept looked upon with favor. Since most communities had a few ne'er-do-wells and indigents who had to be taken care of at public expense, county poorhouses existed, but few greater disgraces could occur to an individual than to be sent to the poorhouse. That danger was held up to youngsters by their elders as the ultimate disaster if they did not cultivate habits of diligence and thrift.

The shame of poverty was recognized by everybody, for it was generally accepted that poverty resulted from an individual's own negligence, laziness, or avoidable incompetence. Hence little sympathy was wasted on any except those who had suffered devastating calamities like blindness or accidents that left them helplessly crippled. For the able-bodied, society's prescription was hard work. In a land of opportunity hard work, it was believed, would lead to independence. The zeal to escape the disgrace of poverty accounts for much of the nineteenth-century insistence on thrift and diligence.

Organized society sought to direct young men in all walks of life to paths that would lead to self-improvement and prosperity. Lectures were established for mechanics and workers, libraries were created especially designed for the needs of ambitious young people, and an enormous amount of useful or inspiring literature was published to stimulate them to improve themselves. In 1831 Edward Everett gave the opening talk at the inauguration in Boston of a series appropriately named the Franklin Lectures. He recalled how Franklin's rise from a printer's apprentice to a man of power and influence illustrated the way in which a young man by the practice of similar diligence could advance in the world. He pointed out for the edification of the young men in his audience that many of the great successes in world history had come "of humble origin, narrow fortune, small advantages, and [were] self-taught."[9]

In 1856, again in Boston, at the unveiling of a monument to Franklin, Robert C. Winthrop once more called upon the working youth of the city to realize what an example they had in Franklin of the way to improve themselves and get ahead in the world:

Behold him, Mechanics and Apprentices, holding out to you an example of diligence, economy, and virtue, and personifying the triumphant success which may await those who follow it! Behold him, ye that are humblest and poorest in present condition or in future prospect. Lift up your heads and look at the image of a man who rose from nothing, who owed nothing to parentage or patronage, who enjoyed no advantages of early education which are not open a hundred fold to yourselves, who performed the most menial services in the business in which his early life was employed, but who lived to stand before kings, and died to leave a name which the world will never forget.[10]

The ambition to get ahead in the world was confined to no group or religion, though it made its greatest appeal and had its most notable effect in the industrial East. Success, of course, was relative and differed in degree from region to region. A farm boy in the hill country of North Carolina, for example, was enjoined to work hard, save enough to buy a few acres for himself, and become independent. His wealth might never exceed the possession of a small farm and its livestock, but he held his head high and knew that he was captain of his own fate. He might sell his farm at a profit and move on to Kentucky or even farther west, where land was cheap and he could improve his status. Such ambition accounted for much of the restless movement from agricultural areas.

A farm boy in Massachusetts might be lured to try his fortune in Boston or some other town where business and industry flourished. New York attracted many farm boys from New England and rural areas of the Middle Atlantic states. Employers in the cities preferred farm boys because they were willing to work harder than city boys and did not object to any task, however lowly. City boys already in the 1820's had a reputation of disdaining certain kinds of work, of loafing on the job, of being impertinent, and of wasting too much on finery. Such characteristics violated the doctrines of thrift and diligence that were the cornerstones of success. Since country boys had no opportunities to learn these shiftless habits, employers welcomed them and took them in as apprentices in various trades and businesses.

A belief arose that the great successes in business were men brought up in the country, and annalists of business pointed out examples to prove their point. For example, Cornelius Vanderbilt, founder of that wealthy family dynasty, left a poor farm on Staten Island to ferry passengers to Manhattan Island. Before the middle of the century he had a monopoly of the New York Harbor ferries and had earned the title of "Commodore" Vanderbilt. When someone in later years asked him how he had accumulated his wealth, he replied, "By working hard and saying nothing about it."

Thomas Mellon was another farm boy who received an inspiration that sent him on his way to wealth. Again it was Benjamin Franklin who stimulated his ambition. As a lad of fourteen, laboring on a farm near Pittsburgh in 1828, young Mellon came upon a copy of Franklin's *Autobiography*, which stirred him to action. "I had not before imagined any other course of life superior to farming," he later reported, "but the reading of Franklin's life led me to question this view. For so poor and friendless a boy to be able to become a merchant or professional man had seemed an impossibility; but here was Franklin, poorer than myself, who by industry, thrift, and frugality had become learned, wise, and elevated to wealth and fame. The maxims of 'Poor Richard' exactly suited my sentiments. . . . I regard the reading of Franklin's *Autobiography* as the turning point of my life."[11] Moving from the farm to Pittsburgh, Mellon became a lawyer, a banker, and the founder of a great financial dynasty.

But Vanderbilt and Mellon were only two out of many farm boys who came to the city and made good, as inspirational writers were fond of pointing out. In 1883 Wilbur F. Crafts, a Brooklyn preacher, investigated the backgrounds of 500 successful Americans in various occupations and discovered that 57 percent of them had been brought up on farms. Only 17 percent of the successes were city-bred. He concluded that if an American wanted to rise to eminence, he "should select a country farm for his birthplace."[12]

Preachers and other moralists decades before Crafts were fond of citing such testimony to prove the success-inducing qualities of farm life, but actually some of the eminent successes in business in the early days of the country got their start elsewhere. For example, the founder of the great Astor fortune, John Jacob Astor, son of a butcher, was a penniless German immigrant when he arrived in New York in 1784 with a few musical instruments to sell. Managing to set up as a small vendor of furs, by 1808 he was head of the newly chartered American Fur Company. Within a few years he had become one of the most important fur traders in America. In 1834 he retired from the American Fur Company, which for most of the past two decades had dominated the fur trade in the United States. In the meantime, Astor had bought up huge blocks of New York real estate, which made his heirs enormously wealthy.

Some men had material success thrust upon them simply because they had the good fortune to settle in a spot where land values increased rapidly. Such was the case of Henry Brevoort, the elder, of New York, who early in the nineteenth century owned a tract of land suitable for a sizable farm between Eighth and Thirteenth streets. To scare boys out of his watermelon patch west of Broadway, he kept a pet bear tethered there. His family had run a truck farm and dairy, and Henry did little else except sit on the land and let its increasing value as city real estate make him rich.

During the early 1830's prosperity seemed to beckon to everybody. Money was easy to borrow, and speculation was rampant. Everywhere men were talking of improvements to come in canals and railroads, and towns and states were floating bonds to pay for all sorts of projects. Since the federal treasury had a surplus from the sale of government lands, Congress passed a bill to distribute some of the federal money to the states. This distribution encouraged further public works and increased inflation. But no boom can last forever, and by the spring of 1837 the blow fell. English banks which had bought up millions of dollars' worth of American bonds raised their interest rates and restricted credit to American borrowers. In the previous summer President Andrew Jackson had issued what was called his Specie Circular, which suspended payment for government land in paper money; henceforth all such payments had to be made in gold or silver. This decree, plus the action of the British bankers, ended the speculative boom and precipitated the celebrated Panic of 1837. The panic brought disaster to businesses and individuals throughout the country. Customers besieged banks, demanding payment in gold or silver, and these runs forced many banks to close their doors. Men who thought they had fortunes in bonds and mortgages found themselves penniless. Factories, unable to sell their products, shut down. The building of many canals and railroads, begun with high hopes only a few months earlier, suddenly stopped. Workers all over the country found themselves without jobs. The streets of the cities were soon swarming with beggars. Hope and optimism which had characterized the country only a year earlier vanished as gloom settled over the land.

The Panic of 1837 caused a depression that lasted into the 1840's. One of the results of this depression was the elimination of many get-rich-quick schemes and the rejection of wildcat promoters, who had flourished in previous years. Some appraisers of the social impact of the period of deflation saw certain good influences to be derived from it. Moralists pointed out that those who had been prudent in their investments, those who had not gone into debt, those who owned farms without mortgages and could sustain themselves, all such cautious and hardworking people could now be an example to others. The lesson to be derived was one of prudence and honesty.

Gradually conditions improved, banks reopened, and the

wheels of industry began once more to turn. But the Panic of 1837 had taught men a lesson that for a time they would remember. Fantastic schemes for easy money and quick success would be less alluring. Many people in the older settled regions who had been ruined by depression were eager to start life afresh. The discouragement of the depression induced many emigrants to set out for Texas and Oregon. Always there was the dream of a new fortune to be made in a fresh land. Americans soon regained their resiliency. Hope may droop but never dies.

The port of Philadelphia at the end of the eighteenth century was the busiest in the new nation. Square-rigged ships from all over the world brought exotic wares to the docks along the Delaware and took on cargoes of forest products and foodstuffs from the rich Pennsylvania hinterlands. Shipwrights are at work in the foreground. *Engraving by William Birch & Son, 1800. Courtesy, Library of Congress.*

Chapter 7

Town Life and
Industrial Work

A visitor reaching any part of the United States in 1790, the date of the first federal census, would have found only six cities with more than 8,000 inhabitants, and the largest of these, Philadelphia, had a population of only 42,520. Unlike the present day, most people lived in the country. In fact, even seventy years later, in 1860, the bulk of the population lived on farms. Young people leaving the farms did not succeed in giving the cities of the United States a greater proportion of the population until 1920.

As the biggest and most prosperous city, Philadelphia enjoyed commerce with the world. Along the docks on the Delaware River a forest of masts swayed above the warehouses on Water Street. Square-rigged vessels laden with goods from Europe, Asia, Africa, or the West Indies emptied cargoes and took on foodstuffs, grain, flour, bacon, hams, salt pork and pickled beef, hides, tanned leather, and forest products, all in demand in the markets across the seas. Coastal vessels brought rice, indigo, rosin, tar, and cotton from South Carolina and Georgia for sale in the north or for transshipment to foreign markets. Craft dock-

Chestnut Street, paved with cobblestones and lined with handsome Georgian houses, testified to the prosperity of Philadelphia. Hitching posts stood along the sidewalk, and pumps provided public drinking water. Sentry boxes housed guards for the State House (Independence Hall, right foreground). Beyond is City Hall, first seat of the U.S. Supreme Court. *Engraving by Birch & Son, 1798. Courtesy, Library of Congress.*

ing from the West Indies gave off a sweet smell of molasses as sweating stevedores rolled out barrels of syrup and casks of sugar. Traffic on Water Street was congested with a tangle of wagons, carts, and handbarrows as laborers trundled the produce of the world to warehouses.

The neat brick houses of Philadelphia's residents, lining shady streets bearing the names of trees—Chestnut, Walnut, Spruce, Pine, Locust, and others—testified to the wealth that trade had brought to the city. High Street, later renamed Market Street, was busier than the others, with covered arcades where tradesmen had their stalls and sold everything from fresh-killed beef to silks and satins which even sober Quaker matrons admired and sometimes bought. The busiest portion of the street was the Jersey Market, two blocks from the waterfront, where small vessels from New Jersey unloaded melons and other fruits, vegetables, meat, poultry, butter, eggs, game, and all the good things to eat produced on the fertile farms of that state.

There in the early morning one could see august businessmen, as well as housewives and servants, with baskets on their arms selecting delicacies for the table from the overflowing stalls. Some dealers specializing in seafood offered all manner of fish from Chesapeake Bay and, in season, oysters, clams, and crabs—favored viands of Philadelphians from the earliest days of settlement.

Philadelphia was a busy and pleasant city where men lived comfortably and grew in prosperity. As wealth accumulated, men built fine houses and furnished them in good taste with the products of the best cabinetmakers of Europe. Philadelphia craftsmen, especially after an influx of skillful Huguenots from France, also learned to turn out excellent furniture, and Philadelphia-made chairs, chests, and tables soon gained a reputation throughout the country. The good taste of Philadelphians set an example for the rest of the country in the early days when the city served as the capital of the nation.

Not only was Philadelphia prosperous, but it was also urbane, cultivated, and interested in the promotion of science and "useful knowledge." The American Philosophical Society, the oldest scientific society in the United States, already enjoyed great prestige, and men like Franklin and Jefferson took pride in the erudition of its members and its contributions to learning. An invitation to join the society was proof that one had arrived intellectually.

The city boasted the most advanced "house of correction," or penitentiary, in the land, the best hospital, a "modern" medical school, and the finest waterworks. It was also proud of its insurance companies. Its volunteer fire companies competed with one another in their eagerness to reach a fire, for the insurance companies gave a bonus to the first to respond.

"The zeal and eagerness with which all Americans fight fires are admirable," commented Médéric Moreau de St.-Méry, a French émigré living in Philadelphia between 1793 and 1798, "but at the same time there are so many willing helpers and there is so little order that they do more harm

Philadelphia was famous for its cabinetmakers, whose handcrafted chairs, chests, and tables are museum pieces today. Shown here are two modern craftsmen in a reconstructed colonial ship, working on the pediment of a highboy with eighteenth-century designs and tools. *Photograph. Courtesy, Colonial Williamsburg.*

"The zeal and eagerness with which all Americans fight fires," observed the French émigré Moreau de St. Méry, sometimes resulted in "more harm than good." *Lithograph by Henry G. Harrison and William N. Weightman, 1858. Courtesy, Library of Congress.*

Philadelphia's waterworks in Centre Square, from which water was piped about the city, was one of the wonders of the early metropolis. *Engraving by Birch & Son, 1800.*

A "fire extinguisher," 1794 style. This leather water bucket, of the type that hung in every Philadelphia household of the period, is now preserved in the Henry Francis du Pont Winterthur Museum near Wilmington, Delaware. *Photograph, courtesy of the Museum.*

than good."[1] The Philadelphia fire companies had an advantage over others in this early period, for the waterworks conveyed water through pipes to most parts of the city—an innovation that excited the admiration of visitors—and the fire engines had hoses with nozzles, which proved more efficient than the bucket brigades which still served at most fires. Each householder was required to keep a few leather buckets hanging on a convenient wall for use in case of fire.

Although Philadelphia was the largest and most prosperous city of the nation at the end of the eighteenth century, life there was not without its trials and dangers. Already urban existence took its toll in human misery. The summers brought the threat of a dreadful plague, yellow fever, which carried off its victims by the hundreds and sent refugees hurrying to the country. No one yet knew that yellow fever was spread by a particular variety of mosquito.

Every inn and many private homes had stables for horses where flies bred by the millions and swarmed into houses, for screens for windows and doors had not yet been invented. Moreau de St.-Méry described the misery that these flies caused. "At table and above all at dessert, they light

The classical influence, widespread in the new Republic, extended even to fire hats reminiscent of Roman helmets, as well as to the architecture of the Philadelphia Water Works (see p. 112). *Courtesy The Henry Francis du Pont Winterthur Museum. Gift of Mrs. Alfred C. Harrison.*

In the days before central heating and modern fire-fighting equipment, fires were an ever-present danger to life and property. They also provided newsworthy spectacles that much of the populace turned out to see. This Currier lithograph was an early equivalent of television coverage of "the great conflagration of December 16 and 17, 1835," in New York, which by that time had hoses and nozzles to equal Philadelphia's. *Courtesy, Library of Congress.*

upon and befoul all food, all drinks," he declared. "They taste everything they see. . . . When a rather large room, hitherto closed, is suddenly opened in the summer, a noise is produced there which imitates that of the sea roaring in the distance; it is the flies who are escaping and cover you as they pass." Flies in bedrooms crawled over the faces of persons trying to sleep in the daytime or woke them at dawn, for they tended to settle down after dark. "Rooms must be kept closed unless one wishes to be tormented in his bed at the break of day, and this need of keeping everything shut makes the heat of the night even more unbearable and sleep more difficult," this French observer lamented.[2] The flies also caused epidemics of typhoid, though the cause of this fever was still unknown. No wonder that residents who could afford to leave Philadelphia—and other cities as well —tried to find relief at the seashore or at cooler country places.

The industries that sprang up in and around Philadelphia were so numerous that they caused wonder in visitors. Moreau de St.-Méry, for example, enumerates in astonishment the multiplicity of manufactories of one kind and an-

A Philadelphia shipyard is shown here in the process of building, in 1799, the 36-gun frigate *Philadelphia*, later captured by Tripolitan pirates and immortalized by the daring exploit of Stephen Decatur in 1804 (see Chapter 3, pp. 50–51). *Engraving by Birch & Son, 1800. Courtesy, Library of Congress.*

other: rope walks for the making of hemp hawsers, thirteen breweries, three distilleries for making whiskey and rum, three makers of playing cards, fifteen potteries, six places for the manufacture of chocolate, thirty-one printing houses, paper mills, chemical plants for making nitric acid, sulfate of soda, and sal ammoniac (ammonium chloride), brickyards, flour mills, three type foundries, cannon foundries, coppersmiths, tinsmiths, hat makers, mills making cut nails, seven gunpowder mills, tanneries, leatherworking shops, and various other small industries, including makers of colors for artists and an ink factory in nearby Germantown.

Philadelphia also had important shipyards for building sailing vessels used in oceanic commerce, as well as in river transport. Shipyards, like the automobile industry today, required subsidiary crafts, including blacksmiths, ironmongers, ship chandlers, and bakers of ship biscuit (hardtack). Moreau de St.-Méry, in his comments on shipbuilding, revealed a European prejudice against American oak, which he claimed rotted more quickly and was more subject to worms than oak grown in the Old World. He also observed that forests around Philadelphia were being destroyed by

Under a spreading chestnut tree,
  The village smithy stands;
The smith, a mighty man is he,
  With large and sinewy hands. . . .

Longfellow's tribute to the black-smith, sold as a ballad with the cover shown here, indicates the smith's social significance in this period. One of the most important craftsmen of the day, he was essential to farmers, shipbuilders, and other industries and was as necessary to the traveling public as filling stations are today. *Lithograph by E. W. Bouvé, 1848. Courtesy, Library of Congress.*

A steam packet in mid-Atlantic. The British steamship *Liverpool*, 464 horsepower and 1,150 tons, is pictured on her maiden voyage to New York in October, 1838. *Lithograph by N. Sarony, published by H. R. Robinson, Wall Street, New York (1838). Courtesy, Library of Congress.*

the greed of builders for convenient timber and the need of the city for firewood.

Important as Philadelphia was at the end of the eighteenth century, it was soon to lose its preeminence in trade —and in population—to New York. Though in 1790 New York had a population of only 33,131, by 1810 it had nearly tripled to 96,000 and surpassed Philadelphia. Manhattan's progress resulted from the convenience of its harbor for vessels coming from Europe, its waterways leading into the interior, and the vigor with which its businessmen pushed trade with other regions of the nation. The lead which New York acquired by 1810 it retained; for the next century and a half it continued to grow in population and prosperity, and only in our time have New York's size and consequent congestion threatened it with disaster.

At the end of the eighteenth and in the early years of the nineteenth century, all was bustle and stir in New York. Ships from the four corners of the earth found berths in the East River, then the principal docking area, for the more exposed Hudson River side was avoided by sailing ships. Not until large transatlantic liners required more turning room did the Hudson River side of Manhattan develop its ocean terminals. The East River, really a strait between New York's Upper Bay and Long Island Sound, had two entrances, one at each end. Ships coming in from the Sound, however, had to brave the treacherous rocks and whirling currents of Hell Gate. During the Revolution a British man-of-war, bringing millions of dollars to pay the king's soldiers, foundered in Hell Gate and sank with all its gold, which has eluded treasure hunters ever since. Despite the danger, however, coastal vessels from New England and sometimes transatlantic ships used Hell Gate passage to reach the East River docks. In the winter, when floating ice from the Hudson clogged the Upper Bay, the Hell Gate route appeared more attractive.

New York strove to improve its shipping throughout the first half of the nineteenth century. Steam navigation, which

117

began with Fulton's *Clermont* on the Hudson in 1807, rapidly expanded after the conclusion in 1815 of the peace treaty with England that ended the War of 1812. Steamboats plying the Hudson and Long Island Sound brought both passengers and goods from the interior and from New England to Manhattan. New York's greatest innovation in shipping, however, was the establishment of regular service to Europe and later to coastal ports with so-called packet ships that departed punctually on schedule, something new for sailing vessels.

New York newspapers in October, 1817, announced that at the first of the coming year, four well-made new vessels would begin regular service between New York and Liverpool. Promptly at 10 A.M. on January 5, 1818, the *James Monroe* hoisted sail for Liverpool. On the previous day the *Courier* had sailed from the English port. Thus began the monthly service of the famous Black Ball Line, so called from the line's symbol, a black ball suspended from the top of the foremast. These fast vessels carried passengers, valuable freight, money, and mail. Their speed and regularity, in comparison with the irregular schedules of previous sailing ships, made them the early-nineteenth-century equivalent of our airlines. They served a highly useful purpose and had little competition until the Cunard Line in 1848 began regular steamship schedules between Liverpool and New York. Thousands of passengers traveled on the packet ships, and many immigrants reached New York in the steerage of these sailing vessels.

By the end of the third decade of the nineteenth century several other packet lines, in addition to the Black Ball, were operating from New York, and shippers could count on weekly sailings. Philadelphia and Baltimore also established packet lines, and for a while one operated from Charleston, South Carolina. Regular sailings from New York to Le Havre improved the service to France. New York particularly and the East Coast generally enjoyed relatively rapid transportation to and from Europe through most of the first half of the nineteenth century.

As in our time, travelers flocked to New York to take ship for Europe. On sailing days the East River docks swarmed with hacks, carriages, and carts bringing well-dressed passengers and their luggage. Horse-drawn vehicles made an even worse tangle of traffic than modern cars and trucks. Through the milling crowds, bleary-eyed sailors, still unsteady from their last night of carousal ashore, staggered toward their ships. On board everything was stir and bustle as last-minute inspection was given to rigging and equipment. Already the salty tang of the sea tempered with the pervasive odor of oakum and tar gave a foretaste of adventure. Going to sea in a sailing ship was a more risky undertaking than a crossing by plane today, and an air of tense excitement permeated the docks on embarkation day.

Packet ships arriving in New York from Europe during the first half of the nineteenth century usually brought a heavy passenger list of emigrants, chiefly from Ireland and Germany. Bearing bundles tied together with cord or heavy valises containing all their earthly possessions, they stumbled ashore, confused and uncertain about the future. Some were met by relatives or friends who had preceded them. Others, friendless and alone, sought shelter in cheap boardinghouses in the waterfront area. Labor agents signed up

The packet ship *Kossuth* discharges its 590 passengers at the foot of Rutger's Slip, New York, in 1851. The hole in the ship's bow was the result of a collision with another packet ship 600 miles out from New York. *Wood engraving in* Gleason's Pictorial Drawing-Room Companion, *June 14, 1851. Courtesy, Library of Congress.*

able-bodied men for work on the canals, on the new railroads, and on other construction projects where brawn rather than skill was required. This was the day before the steam shovel and earth-moving machinery, when excavation had to be done manually with pick and shovel or with a drag pan pulled by a mule. The country needed laborers, and Ireland—and, to a lesser degree, Germany—supplied them. Some of the Germans, with crafts and special skills, found better jobs. A scattering of emigrants from other countries also arrived on the packet ships, but the mass movement from Scandinavia and Central and Southern Europe had not yet begun. Nevertheless, New York, which even in colonial times had a variety of foreign types, was becoming the most polyglot region of the nation. The sound of strange tongues heard in the East River section and its boardinghouses already was making New York a veritable Tower of Babel.

The opening of the Erie Canal in 1825 brought cargoes of grains, meat, flour, hides, potash, pearl ash, and other bulky freight from the Great Lakes region. These last-named commodities were by-products of forest clearing; when trees were burned, the ash became a source of raw chemicals. Water poured through casks of hardwood ashes leached out lye which, when boiled down into a salt, was called potash. If this was heated in a kiln, the product was known as pearl ash. Every housewife needed lye for boiling with fat to make soap, potash was used in glassmaking, and developing industries in the East had other uses for these chemicals.

Shrewd New Yorkers also developed a profitable trade with the South. Bankers, by offering credit to Southern cotton planters, frequently obtained a lien on crops before they were even planted. Stout sailing ships able to round stormy Cape Hatteras with a minimum of risk gathered up cotton bales from Charleston, Mobile, and even New Orleans and brought them to New York for transshipment to Europe. The same vessels carried to the South cargoes of luxury

By the mid-nineteenth century New York's sophisticated pleasures included such gilded spas as this Broadway "refreshment saloon." Note the elegant spittoon at corner of the bar. *Wood engraving in* Gleason's, *May 15, 1852. Courtesy, Library of Congress.*

goods, hardware, and foodstuffs that cotton planters were unwilling to produce for sale in the Southern markets. Thus New York made a profit from interest on loans, on freight charged the planters, and on the markup of goods sold to the South. The lack of enterprise in the South helped enrich New York.

During the period before the Civil War, Southern planters and their wives enjoyed making a trip to New York for both business and pleasure. The planters could talk business and politics with their agents (called factors), negotiate loans, and enjoy the exotic pleasures of a beginning metropolis unlike any other American city. Their wives could revel in shops filled with the luxuries of Europe or inveigle their husbands into evenings of music or the theater. For many, New York was becoming an attraction as alluring as a trip to Europe. Its appeal increased throughout the nineteenth century as restaurants, concert halls, and museums multiplied.

Though not so easy, shopping in New York and other urban centers was perhaps more interesting in this period than it is today. The department store with its carefully

121

As apothecary shops evolved into "drug stores" later in the century, they began to diversify their wares to include a soda fountain—literally for soda water (right)—and cosmetic creams such as "Pond's Extra" (center background). *Lithograph by Roy, 1880. Courtesy, Library of Congress.*

organized divisions had not yet developed. Most stores, even in such up-and-coming cities as New York, were still general stores selling everything from hardware to hard candy in a glorious jumble, the sort of array that one now sees re-created in "country stores" at tourist centers. With the exception of apothecary shops, which evolved into drugstores, few stores confined themselves to specialties. A general store would have dry goods and notions at one end and staple groceries at the other. Most perishable foodstuffs, however, were handled in markets where vendors maintained stalls. There one sought meat, vegetables, fruits, and seafood.

New York's excellent markets impressed visitors. Moreau de St.-Méry, for example, was astonished at the abundance of fish and game in what was called, perhaps unfortunately, the Fly Market, at the foot of Maiden Lane. "In the market you can get sixty-three sorts of fish, as well as oysters, lobsters, sea- and fresh-water crabs, crawfish, fresh- and salt-water prawns, eight other sorts of shellfish, turtles. There are fifty-two varieties of animals, game, kid, bear, o'possum, hare, rabbits, etc."[3]

The city with the oldest traditions in the United States was Boston, and it never let the rest of the country forget its ancient importance. But Boston allowed New York and other cities to outstrip it in shipping and business enterprise. In 1790 it was the third city in population with 18,038 inhabitants. By 1820, with a population of 43,298, it had

Beacon Hill, long the residential area of Boston's cultural leaders, was once as high as the Massachusetts State House (right). The hill, named for a beacon that stood at its peak, was gradually graded down, as shown here, and the gravel used to fill Mill Cove, site of today's North Station. *Lithograph by John H. Bufford, 1858, after a drawing by J. R. Smith, 1811–12.*

fallen to fourth place with Baltimore ahead of it with 62,738; at this time New York had a population of 123,-706.

One reason for Boston's lack of business enterprise may have been the caution of its business leaders. Robert G. Albion in *The Rise of New York Port* cites a work attributing Boston's loss of initiative to "the so-called 'spendthrift trust' whereby cautious merchant fathers tied up their sons' inheritances in trust funds which assured a comfortable income but prevented the use of the principal."[4] This produced coupon cutters with time for literature, music, and the arts but deprived many Boston men of venture capital for new enterprises. At any rate, Boston became the cultural leader among American cities, even surpassing Philadelphia, while New York outdid them all in commerce and finance. Between 1850 and 1860 New York's foreign trade was six times that of all New England, Albion points out.[5]

Nevertheless, New England, like Scotland, had one important export that affected the rest of the nation: its men. New Englanders went out to all parts of the country and demonstrated their skill and acumen in business. For example, their invasion of New York was so great that New Yorkers, led by Washington Irving, organized the St. Nicholas Society to offset the New England Society, which spent its efforts glorifying the past deeds of that region. Many ship

123

The literary interests of Bostonians is apparent in this view of Fetridge & Co.'s Periodical Arcade at Washington and State streets, Boston. The number of children in the picture is indicative of a continuing tradition. *Wood engraving in* Gleason's, *July 31, 1852. Courtesy, Library of Congress.*

captains commanding vessels from New York were New Englanders and were some of the city's most influential merchants and financiers.

It is significant that the New England Society in New York, among its objectives, stated an intention "to establish and maintain a library." Bostonians, even those away from home, expected to retain and cultivate their literary interests. During most of the nineteenth century Boston was the literary capital of the United States, and book publishing was one of its most significant industries. It also had excellent bookshops. If one wanted a book, old or new, the best hope of finding it was in Boston. If Boston was complacent about its intellectual accomplishments, it had some right to be.

South of Philadelphia, Baltimore was the fastest-growing and most enterprising city. Its prosperity depended on a network of roads that it opened to tap the fertile farmlands of Maryland and even the Shenandoah Valley. Its port handled large cargoes of grain, flour, pork, and beef, which had an increasing demand in the West Indies, Latin America, and Europe. In 1805 an English traveler visiting Ellicott

Mills near Baltimore observed that they could turn out 300 barrels of flour each day; many mills in the region supplied Baltimore's export houses with flour for the West Indian and Latin American trade, which grew with the passing years. Other foodstuffs from the farms of Maryland and adjacent territory poured into Baltimore for shipment abroad.

Urban development south of Baltimore lagged in the first half of the nineteenth century, for the South was primarily an agricultural region with few industries. Charleston, South Carolina, which had been relatively more important in colonial times, allowed much of its commerce to be drained away by New York, Baltimore, and Philadelphia. Savannah was a sleepy, though pleasant, little town. Annapolis, in Maryland, and Williamsburg, in Virginia, which had been of some consequence in colonial times, remained museum pieces. Norfolk, burned at the beginning of the American Revolution and rebuilt as an ugly town of wooden houses, was a useful port chiefly for the shipment of tobacco. Alexandria, Virginia, a small town on the banks of the Potomac, attained some fame as a shipping point for its

The flourishing port of Baltimore shipped a great deal of flour and grain from the farmlands of Maryland and Virginia's Shenandoah Valley. *Aquatint by W. J. Bennett, 1831. Courtesy, Library of Congress.*

A typical Maryland flour mill of the early period, operated by waterpower. Most small county mills of this type had been superseded by more efficient plants by the time this sketch was made in 1863. *Pencil drawing by Edwin Forbes. Courtesy, Library of Congress.*

excellent flour. Early in the nineteenth century Richmond was beginning to grow, and by 1860 it had become a city with a few important industries, including an ironworks capable of turning out artillery for the Confederate armies.

The greatest urban developments before 1860 occurred in the interior of the country, where towns strategically situated took advantage of the growing traffic on rivers and lakes connected by a network of canals, turnpikes, and the expanding railroads. For example, Rochester, New York, which in 1816 had only about 100 houses but already boasted a cotton mill, flour mills, and several inns for transients, within two decades had become an important inland center of trade and industry, thanks to the opening of the Erie Canal and the improvement of other transportation. By the middle of the century it had become the most important flour-milling center in the country.

In similar fashion, other cities profited from improved transportation. The milling of grains and meat-packing were the most important of the early industries, for the farms of the backcountry produced vast quantities of corn, wheat, barley, rye, hogs, and cattle. Some of the grain found its way to distilleries and was condensed into whiskey, for whiskey was more easily transported than the bulky grain. Canalboats carried many barrels of whiskey bound for Eastern saloons. Buffalo and Cleveland on the Great Lakes, like Cincinnati and Louisville on the Ohio River, grew rapidly in the first half of the century. Grain processing and meat-packing were important in their development. By 1860 Chicago, with more than 100,000 inhabitants, was already giving promise of becoming the metropolis of the Middle West. St. Louis became the most important supply point for fur traders and emigrants headed for the West; it received an enormous impetus after the discovery of gold in California. Pittsburgh, early noted for both its whiskey and its iron, grew rapidly after 1830 as a producer of iron and steel. New Orleans, long the shipping point for produce floated down the Ohio and Mississippi river systems, by 1850 had more than 116,000 inhabitants and was the most colorful and exotic of all American cities, mingling elements of French, Spanish, American, and African cultures.

One of the most profitable of early American industries was shipbuilding, for in the days of wooden ships American forests supplied ample materials near the seashore. Until iron ships made wooden vessels obsolete, New England from Maine to Connecticut was lined with shipyards turning out craft of an infinite variety, from small whaleboats to great square-riggers capable of a voyage around Cape Horn. Few seaport towns were so small that they could not boast enough shipwrights to man at least a small

A view of St. Louis, supply point for fur traders and Western emigrants, as it looked in the 1830's, when the artist George Catlin traveled up the Missouri in the steamer *Yellowstone* (foreground). *Painting by Catlin, 1839. Courtesy, Smithsonian Institution.*

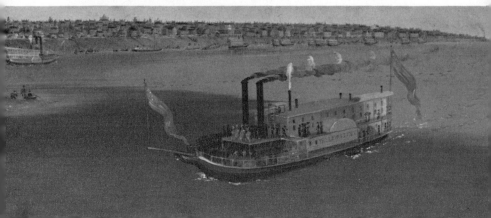

yard. One should remember that the building of a wooden ship was a relatively simple operation though it required the knowledge and skills of good craftsmen.

New England shipwrights, famous for their dexterity and know-how, produced vessels that outsailed most others and were noted for their speed, ease of handling, and seaworthiness. Furthermore, New England's yards were so efficient that in spite of higher wages, they could build a 500-ton vessel for $37,500 as against a cost of $43,000 in England.

The ultimate attainment in American ship construction was reached with the building of the clipper ships, trim and fast, carrying a veritable cloud of canvas. In fact, one of the most famous was named the *Flying Cloud*. Designed for long voyages, clipper ships were used in the China trade and in voyages around Cape Horn to California. Their speed was phenomenal; one clipper made the trip from San Francisco to New York in eighty days; another took only eighty-four days from Canton to New York. Small wonder that on a fine day crowds lined the Battery in New York and cheered as these ships with all sails set stood out to sea. The quality of the ships also helps account for the eagerness with which New England boys signed on for long voyages.

In the days before steam, the sources of waterpower determined the location of many industries. The earliest industries requiring power-driven machinery were sawmills and gristmills, located on streams where dams could be

The prosperous Mississippi port of New Orleans by the mid-century boasted a population exceeding 116,000—the most colorful mixture of French, Spanish, African, and "American" in the country. *Lithograph by Otto Onken, 1851.* Courtesy, Library of Congress.

A shipyard in East Boston in the clipper ship days. The Boston State House and Bunker Hill Monument can be seen on the horizon. *Wood engraving in* Ballou's Pictorial Drawing-Room Companion, *May 19, 1855. Courtesy, Library of Congress.*

The name of this clipper ship, the *Oriental*, is indicative of the Chinese trade in which she was engaged. *Wood engraving in* Gleason's, *September 18, 1852. Courtesy, Library of Congress.*

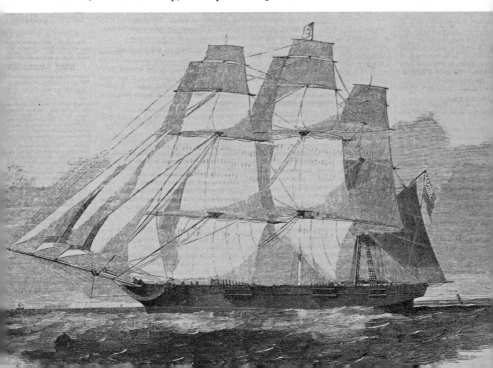

built and water deflected through flumes to turn huge wheels; these transmitted power through gears to the machinery of the mills. The best streams were creeks and rivers with a rapid fall so that a sequence of dams could be built. New England with a fall line (the beginning of rapids) not far inland had ideal situations for water-driven mills. Brandywine Creek in Delaware was another excellent location for flour mills; there the first DuPont powder factories also found adequate waterpower for their purposes. All along the East Coast, streams soon were lined with mills of various types.

During the colonial period and even later, many textiles were made in the home by women who spun yarn of wool, flax, or cotton on their spinning wheels and, with the help of men weavers, produced cloth on their own looms. But after the Revolution, textile machinery, invented in England, was smuggled into the United States, and the first spinning and weaving mills were established. Before the turn of the century, small cotton mills were started in Philadelphia and at a number of places in New England and New Jersey. But the disruption of trade during the Napoleonic Wars, the Embargo Act imposed by Jefferson in 1807 preventing trade with Europe, and the War of 1812 forced Americans to manufacture their own cloth on a larger scale or go naked.

During the War of 1812 Providence, Rhode Island, counted 169 small spinning and weaving plants in the vicinity. Textiles had become a flourishing industry, but the dumping of British goods after the war ruined many of the mills. British competition precipitated in 1816 a protective tariff which taxed imported fabrics 25 percent of their value and permitted American mills in time to regain their prosperity. In 1793 a clever Yankee inventor, Eli Whitney, had developed a machine for separating cotton from the seed, an operation that previously had been done laboriously by hand. This invention greatly accelerated the use of cotton both in this country and abroad. The use of cotton cloth

130

A cutaway view of a flour mill on Brandywine Creek, Delaware, showing gears attached to the water wheel and the various steps in grinding, sifting the bran from the flour, and finally storing the flour in barrels. *Photograph of a working model in the Hagley Mills Museum. Courtesy, Eleutherian Mills Historical Library.*

and the consequent demand for it increased enormously in the next two decades.

One of the most famous of the early cotton mills, at Lowell, Massachusetts, on the Merrimack River, drew comments from many foreign visitors, amazed at the management's paternal oversight of hundreds of girls who made up the work force. A Frenchman, Michael Chevalier, who visited Lowell in 1834, described the operation of the mills which employed some 6,000 operatives, nearly 5,000 of them girls from seventeen to twenty-four years of age. Drawn from New England farms, they were happy at the opportunity to save a tidy sum in two or three years, when they usually quit to get married. Chevalier was impressed by their freshness, neatness, and reticent deportment, unlike anything he knew in France. "In France it would be difficult to conceive of a state of things in which young girls, generally pretty, should be separated from their families, fifty to a hundred miles from home, in a town in which their parents could have no one to advise and watch over them," he commented.[6] Their parents did not have to worry, for the management built dormitories for the girls, hired matrons, and saw to it that the girls lived exemplary lives. Indeed, there was little time for anything else, for they

Factory workers by the 1860's were less cheerful than the "Lowell girls" of an earlier period. *This illustration, "Bell Time," from Harper's Weekly for July 25, 1868, was engraved from a drawing by the well-known painter Winslow Homer. Courtesy, Library of Congress.*

worked from dawn to dark in the wintertime and for thirteen and a half hours in the summer; the average workweek was seventy hours. Yet English observers, Anthony Trollope among them, regarded the Lowell mills as a veritable industrial utopia compared with mills in Manchester, England.

The truth is that hard work was regarded in this period as the lot of man—and of woman—and the girls in the Lowell mills were happy to find relief from even harder work that was the lot of the average woman condemned to household drudgery. Countless visitors, taken to Lowell as one of the sights of the country, commented on the happiness of the girls and the eagerness of others to find jobs in textile mills. None felt that it was demeaning to be a factory worker. Girls wrote home about their pleasant surroundings, the lectures provided by the management, and the church services they were expected to attend on Sunday. The notion that this sort of paternalism was wicked had not yet dawned on anybody's consciousness.

Not all mills were as humanitarian as the Lowell mills, and some imposed longer hours in less pleasant surroundings. Others discovered that many operations could be performed by children, and it was not uncommon to find six-year-olds tending spinning machines. In many cases mills employed whole families and put everybody to work. In 1832 a report made in Boston declared that two-fifths of the workers in the textile mills were children. Their ages ranged from six to seventeen.

Yet long hours and rigid supervision of behavior, such as prevailed at Lowell, did not discourage girls all over New England from seeking work in mills. The depression that occurred in 1837, however, threw many out of work and lowered wages. An influx of Irish emigrants into New England also introduced a new competition for jobs and permitted millowners to keep wages low, cut costs, and eliminate such amenities as they had previously provided for their work force. From 1840 to the beginning of the Civil

By the 1850's New England textile mills had taken on the appearance of modern factories. Lowell, Massachusetts, with its Boott Cotton Mills pictured here, gloried in being called "the Manchester of America." *Wood engraving in Gleason's, May 29, 1852. Courtesy, Library of Congress.*

War working conditions in industry, especially in New England, deteriorated.

Industrialization in the first half of the nineteenth century accounted for the rapid urbanization of several regions, notably New England. While Boston let New York and other cities outstrip it in foreign commerce, it developed numerous satellite towns engaged in the manufacture of shoes, hardware, hats, clocks, brassware, stoves, sewing machines, and countless other products needed by the growing country. Other areas, it is true, developed industries, but New England, because of its waterpower, ingenious craftsmen, and lack of fertile land for agriculture, took the lead and became the paramount industrial region of the United States before 1860.

City life, even in the heaviest population centers like New York, was very different from life in a big city today. In some ways life was pleasanter; in others it was more difficult. Many of the services that we take for granted were nonexistent. No telephones made communication easy. Messengers bearing written notes carried invitations to social affairs and to funerals. Unwholesome as we think our cities

Independence Day, or the Fourth of July, was a great occasion for young and old in the new nation. The firecrackers were imported from China. *Lithograph published by C. H. Brainard, 1859. Courtesy, Library of Congress.*

are, congested areas before the Civil War were infinitely worse. Hogs roamed at large, even in New York, acting as scavengers of garbage thrown in the streets. In Washington, the capital of the nation, a stinking canal occupied part of what is now Constitution Avenue, and butchers threw their offal into it. Numerous stables for carriage horses, as noted earlier, bred flies which afflicted every town. Many householders in cities felt a necessity of keeping a cow or two to provide fresh milk, and from time to time even Presidents of the United States insisted on a cow on the White House grounds to ensure a supply of wholesome milk. Transportation was also a problem for the average citizen, who could not afford to keep a horse and carriage. Horse-drawn hacks supplied the place of modern taxis but they were slow, and the dusty—or muddy—streets made getting around less than pleasant at almost any time of the year. Runaway horses also added to the hazards of life on city streets.

Yet despite trials and annoyances encountered in cities, many residents found life there preferable to the isolation of life on farms. Human beings as a whole are gregarious and enjoy the society of one another. Cities provided more opportunities for social contacts. The well-to-do could arrange receptions, dinner and theater parties, and other occasions for meetings with their kind. Less affluent folk found ample opportunities for socializing at church festivals, school assemblies, and other gatherings, including funerals. Political rallies and parades were part of city life that supplied excitement and entertainment. The Fourth of July in particular was the occasion for speeches, picnics, and fireworks that appealed to both young and old. Because hard work absorbed much youthful energy, juvenile delinquency was then rarer in the cities, and one could walk the streets with greater safety. City life in this period was not without its compensations.

Chapter 8

Farms and Plantations— Varied Life in the Country

Although the gradual drift to towns and cities gained momentum in the first half of the nineteenth century, the vast majority of people, both North and South, remained country dwellers. Even as late as 1860 the population of the cities numbered only 6,216,518, while the country was occupied by 25,226,803 souls. We were a nation of farmers and those engaged in related activities. Although today the United States still produces enormous crops, the invention of intricate laborsaving machinery and the mechanizing of agriculture have made the individual farm laborer less essential. Furthermore, no longer can the small farmer by the labor of his own hands and those of his immediate family compete successfully with the big capitalistic enterprises that have taken over most farming activities. Thus in our time conditions in the country have vastly changed, and thousands of small farms are now deserted.

Before the Civil War, however, with the exception of the slave-labor plantations in the South, farming offered every man an opportunity for free enterprise, the hope of success, and a chance to improve his economic status. American farmers were the most independent workers in the world, and politicians, if they expected to win elections, made certain to appeal to their special interests. Even yet, political oratory and political action retain many clichés from the day when farmers were the largest group in the land.

Farms varied widely in type and size in the different regions of the country. In New England most farms were small, for, with the exception of the Connecticut Valley and portions of Rhode Island, much of the land was rocky and less fertile than other parts of the country. New York had great estates in the Hudson Valley and numerous smaller farms. New Jersey had both small farms and large plantations. Pennsylvania was a region of fertile farms, many of the best owned and cultivated by hardworking Germans. In the mountain valleys of Maryland the same German types had cleared land and owned prosperous farms; in the tidewater regions large plantations worked by slave labor predominated. The same was true of the coastal regions of Virginia, North and South Carolina, and Georgia. In the up-country of these states, however, small farms prevailed, many of them owned and worked by Scotch-Irish settlers with a scattering of Germans. Many German families, for example, had moved into the Shenandoah Valley and filtered down into the Carolinas.

As soil in tidewater regions became exhausted, some slaveholders bought estates in the up-country or moved to fresh land in the West and Southwest, Kentucky, Tennessee, Alabama, and Mississippi. Before the middle of the century a migration across the Mississippi of both small farmers and slaveowning planters was taking place. Slaveowners chose the Southwest and Missouri, while others took up land in Kansas and the Northwest. The search for rich farmlands became an obsession, the dream of bettering themselves sent thousands of migrants westward, and speculators found in real estate a major outlet for their activities.

The small farms surrounding the growing towns of New England supplied foodstuffs for the townsmen. Corn and hay for the livery stables and private owners of carriage horses were in constant demand, and these two most easily grown crops became a source of ready cash. Nearly every farm also produced a quantity of garden truck, vegetables of all sorts. Even though town dwellers in this period frequently had vegetable gardens of their own, they could not raise enough cabbage, potatoes, peas, onions, and roasting ears of corn to supply all their needs. Nearly every farm raised some poultry: chickens, ducks, geese, or turkeys. The sale of eggs frequently provided the farmer's wife a tiny income called pin money. Farm orchards supplied apples and pears, with cider, both sweet and hard, as a profitable by-product. Cider was the favorite beverage of New England, and Harvard students, for example, demanded cider with their breakfasts. Dairy and beef cattle, hogs, sheep, and occasionally goats were frequently raised. Most farms produced a little of everything that could be easily grown, for they were primarily designed for subsistence, supplying the farmer and his family with necessities ranging from food to clothing. From homegrown flax, linen was made, and a few sheep supplied wool for suits and blankets. Any surplus found a ready market in the towns. Farmers often paid their bills in kind—that is, by bartering produce for goods or services. Many a New England doctor received a bushel of apples or a few brace of ducks for his attention to rural patients.

The small farmers of New England were thrifty and diligent. They added to their incomes by cutting firewood and hauling it to town markets, for stoves and fireplaces were insatiable. Housewives preferred pine, fir, or birchwood for their cookstoves, for these made quick fires which could be regulated more easily than fires of hardwood. The day when a kitchen could boast a gas, oil, or electric stove was still far distant. Chopping stovewood both in town and country was a normal chore for boys, and even the smallest lads could be drafted to "bring in wood" for the kitchen woodbin, which seemed forever empty. Supplying firewood provided an important source of ready money for farmers in New England and other regions accessible to towns.

New England farmers were adept at many crafts. During long winter days when outdoor labor was impossible, they turned out woodenware, made shoes, or sometimes worked at looms weaving woolen blankets or homespun suitings. The early shoe factories at Braintree and other towns sent out piecework, and much stitching and finishing of shoes were done in farmhouses. In slack seasons farmers might do a bit of carpentry or work for a time in the shipyards. The ingenuity of Yankee farmers was proverbial. Many of the farmers' daughters found work in the growing number of textile mills in the region.

Conditions in the Connecticut Valley were somewhat different, for there the soil was rich and farms were larger. The proximity to numerous towns, the growing demand for food, and the ease with which the alluvial land could be cultivated encouraged the planting of root crops, potatoes, turnips, and onions. Rank growths of hay and grains gave rise to the fattening of beef cattle; by-products of the large production of beef were the tanning of hides and the sale of leather to the shoe and harness factories in the region. By 1840 tobacco had become another important crop in the Connecticut Valley. Americans were inveterate cigar smokers, and the Connecticut Valley supplied, as it still does, a particular kind of tobacco used for the outer wrapping of cigars.

Immigrant laborers, avoiding the slave regions of the South, found employment on Connecticut Valley farms. These were among the first in the North to become specialized, with an emphasis on one or two particular products. Dairies and pens for fattening beef cattle supplanted old general-purpose farms where a few cows had been kept. Tobacco growing became the specialty of many others. Some of the alien workers saved their money and in time became prosperous landowners.

Since colonial times the flatlands of Rhode Island had

140

developed a plantation type of agriculture. Stock raising had for many years been an important source of revenue. During colonial times horses in large numbers had been shipped from Rhode Island to the West Indies, and horses continued to be profitable. Early in the nineteenth century, however, preeminence in horse breeding passed to Kentucky, which became famous for its saddle and racehorses. Other livestock found a place on Rhode Island farms, and the pickling of beef and pork for the merchant marine was a farm industry.

New York, New Jersey, and Pennsylvania produced enormous quantities of corn, wheat, barley, oats, and a variety of other food crops, including fruit. In the days before the canning and freezing of fruits and vegetables, farm women dried them in vast quantities. Even yet in the Pennsylvania-Dutch country one can find such unusual items as green corn dried. Tons of apples and pears were peeled, sliced, and dried, as were figs and peaches. These items were sold in commerce, and whaling and other ships carried dried fruit as a relief from too much "salt horse," as the pork and beef on shipboard were described.

Stock raising on the large farms of New York and particularly in Pennsylvania added to the agricultural income of the country. When grain could not be easily transported from regions having no waterways or railroads, it could be fed to cattle, hogs, and sheep, and the animals could be driven to market over any sort of trail. During the first half of the nineteenth century, roads were filled with herds of livestock guided by professional drovers. A traveler could usually spot a herd in the distance by the swirling cloud of dust they kicked up. Certain inns were set up to appeal to these drovers, just as truck drivers today have certain favorite hamburger stands along the highways.

Tough, hard-drinking and loud-swearing, dusty and sweaty, drovers were not welcome guests at the better inns, which had no corrals for their cattle, sheep, or hogs. Livestock on the march, with their less-than-attractive human

141

custodians, did not add to the amenities of the road in the early days of the last century.

Western Pennsylvania produced great quantities of corn and rye. Since it was too bulky to be transported over the mountains at a profit, the Scotch-Irish farmers of the region set up distilleries and turned their grain into whiskey. Many bushels of grain could be condensed into a few jugs and barrels of hard liquor, which was everywhere in demand. For whiskey was virtually a universal drink in nineteenth-century America. Furthermore, it was a useful medium of exchange and often served in lieu of money. Even preachers sometimes received part of their pay in whiskey, which they could barter or drink according to their dispositions. In this fashion some Western farmers solved the problem of the costly transportation of grain.

German and other foreign immigrants, as well as native Americans, moving into the states of Ohio, Michigan, Illinois, Indiana, Minnesota, Iowa, and Kansas, opened up enormous new areas for farming. Wheat, corn, hogs, and cattle, the chief products of these farms, added immensely to the nation's supply of food for home consumption and for export. America was the best-fed nation on earth. These farmers were independent and self-reliant, willing to work hard themselves and to pay well for hired labor. An immigrant need not lack for work with adequate pay in these developing agricultural areas.

The farmers of the Northwest had deliberately avoided the South because of the competition with slave labor. Slavery was a curse which had afflicted the South since colonial times, when settlers tried to solve the vexed problem of an adequate supply of labor by importing slaves from Africa. Always America suffered from a dearth of both manual and skilled workers. In the sixteenth and seventeenth centuries the holding of men in slavery, regardless of race or origin, was accepted as a matter of course. Wealthy Italian merchants, for example, had long been accustomed to order a shipment of household servants, white slaves, from their agents in one of the Eastern European countries. The traffic in human beings was as old as civilization.

In 1619 a Dutch ship brought the first load of Africans to Virginia and sold them to the settlers. That was the beginning of a traffic that was to bequeath to America calamities untold for centuries to come. African slavery, however, did not become an important factor in the North American colonies until late in the seventeenth century, when an English corporation, the Royal African Company, headed by the Duke of York, later King James II, began to push slaves upon the colonists.

Planters maintained that blacks from Africa could endure the steaming rice fields of South Carolina and the sultry tobacco plantations of Virginia much better than white servants, some of whom were bond servants working out four- to seven-year contracts. African slavery looked like the answer to the labor problem, and only here and there did men's consciences bother them about an institution so universally accepted that even theologians found reasons to justify it.

The slave trade proved profitable to American merchants and shipping interests. Makers of rum in Boston, Newport, and other New England towns discovered that a cargo of rum could be exchanged on the west coast of Africa for a shipload of slaves who could be sold at a profit in the West Indies. There the profits could be invested in sugar and molasses, the raw materials for more rum. Thus was established the famous triangular trade with Africa, which benefited African kings with slaves to sell, New England distillers and shippers, and West Indian sugar planters. Soon some of the slaves were brought to the mainland of North America, where they proved to be useful workers. Even that most pious of New England preachers, Cotton Mather, was not above buying a slave, and many preachers argued that bringing heathen souls to Christian lands where they could hear the message of salvation and achieve eternal life was a work of virtue. To exchange present liberty for eternal life in heaven was a bargain, the preachers argued. Only here and there a Quaker or some other troubled soul, Samuel Sewall, the colonial diarist, being one, tried to point out the iniquity of the traffic.

By the end of the eighteenth century African slavery had been so firmly established in the agricultural regions of the South that the Founding Fathers could not eliminate it from the new nation. Thomas Jefferson, though a slaveowner, realized the wickedness of the traffic and would have banned slavery had he been able. More than half a century later, in a speech at Springfield, Illinois, on July 17, 1858, Abraham Lincoln commented on the tragic dilemma of slavery:

> When our government was established, we had the institution of slavery among us. We were in a certain sense compelled to tolerate its existence. It was a sort of necessity. We had gone through our struggle, and secured our own independence. The framers of the Constitution found the institution of slavery amongst their other institutions at the time. They found that by an effort to eradicate it they might lose much of what they had already gained. They were obliged to bow to the necessity.

The South itself was now enslaved by a system that was to be its ruin.

Rice had become one of the most important crops in the coastal region of South Carolina and Georgia. It flourished in rich swamplands which had to be flooded at certain seasons. White men could not endure the pestilential marshes thick with malarial mosquitoes, but it was widely believed that Africans had an immunity that made it possible for them to tend the rice fields and stay healthy. The rice planters saw no solution for their labor problem except African slavery. Slaves were also useful in the pine forests of the Carolinas and Georgia where rosin was collected for distil-

144

An auction in the Rotunda at New Orleans: Pictures, slaves, and estates are being offered for sale to the highest bidder. *Engraving by J. M. Starling in James S. Buckingham,* The Slave States of America, *1842. Courtesy, Library of Congress.*

lation into turpentine and tar needed as ship stores.

Much earlier, slaves had become essential on the sugar-cane plantations of the West Indies, and when Louisiana expanded its sugar industry in the first third of the nineteenth century, the demand increased for African labor. Work on the sugar plantations was hard, and planters in the upper South would frighten recalcitrant slaves by threatening to sell them "down the river" to work in Louisiana.

Despite the need for African slaves on rice and sugar plantations, slavery eventually might have ended because of the expense of the system had it not been for an enormous upsurge in the demand for cotton. Until near the end of the eighteenth century cotton was expensive because of the difficulty of separating the lint from the seeds, especially in the variety known as upland cotton. The lint of sea-island cotton was more easily separated, but it would grow at only a few places on the coast. In any case, the lint had to be picked off the seeds by hand, a process so tedious that a slave could separate only about a pound a day.

A revolution came in 1793, when Eli Whitney, a Yankee schoolmaster from Yale serving as a tutor in the family of General Nathanael Greene in Georgia, invented a machine equipped with rollers, pins, and brushes which would tear cotton fibers from the seeds with speed and efficiency. A small hand-turned gin could produce 50 pounds of lint in a day; a larger gin, operated with waterpower, could turn out 1,000 pounds in the same length of time. A new day was about to dawn for cotton planters—and the prosperity that the gin would bring to the planters would fix slavery even more irrevocably upon the South, where thousands of hands would be required in the cotton fields.

The story of Whitney's struggles to protect his patent is long and involved. Because his gin was a simple mechanism, easily built, mechanics all over the South were soon infringing his patent. At last South Carolina paid him $50,000 for the privilege of reproducing his gins, and he managed to collect other smaller sums.

The multiplication of gins solved the problem of the production of seed-free cotton fibers. Improved spinning and weaving machinery in England had already created an ever-increasing demand for cotton. Since the plantations of the South could now sell at a handsome profit all the cotton they could grow, the first half of the nineteenth century saw an immense expansion of cotton farming. Planters moved into lower Alabama and Mississippi, where the rich alluvial soil was ideally adapted to cotton. They continued their march across the Mississippi to establish more cotton plantations in Arkansas. From there they pushed on into cotton-growing lands in Texas, at first a part of Spanish America, later Mexican, and after 1836 a free republic until its annexation by the United States in 1845. Cotton plantations, and with them slavery, flourished throughout these enormous territories.

The wealthier cotton, rice, and cane planters created an aristocratic society that has gathered about it many romantic myths, partly true, partly false. The legendary picture is one of white-columned houses occupied by beautiful women and courtly men who spent their time in genteel pleasures. Their house servants were smiling, gracious, and perfectly trained. Gangs of cheerful field hands tended the crops and might in the evenings serenade their masters or entertain their guests with dancing or the singing of spirituals. So runs the legend as transmitted by the magnolia-scented school of fiction.

The facts were usually far different. Though beautiful women and courtly men did exist in the South, many of them were troubled by the "peculiar institution," as slavery was designated at the time. Patriots of the Revolutionary period realized that talk of all men being "free and equal" rang false when thousands of Africans were held as human chattels. Patrick Henry, for example, wrote to a friend: "Would anyone believe that I am master of slaves of my own purchase! I am drawn along by the general inconveni-

Eli Whitney's first cotton gin looked very much like the primitive mechanism illustrated here. Such a small, hand-operated model could turn out 50 pounds of lint a day, as against one pound per person per day when separated by hand. *Wood engraving in* Harper's Weekly, December 18, 1869, after a drawing by William L. Sheppard. Courtesy, Library of Congress.

The invention of the cotton gin, combined with improvements in spinning and weaving machinery, led to an enormous expansion of cotton farming throughout the South and Southwest. Pictured here is a typical cotton plantation on the Mississippi River, which provided easy transportation to the outside world. *Currier & Ives lithograph, 1884, after W. A. Walker. Courtesy, Library of Congress.*

ence of living without them. I will not, I cannot justify it. . . . I believe a time will come when an opportunity will be offered to abolish this lamentable evil."[1] This was the dilemma in which Southerners found themselves. Many slaveholders regarded the institution as evil, but they were trapped in it by the need for labor, the economic investment that it represented, and their inability to find a solution. If they freed their slaves, who would work the rice, cotton, and cane fields, and what would become of the freedmen? So slavery remained, and in time, as abolitionists agitated for emancipation, controversialists arose to argue the justification of human bondage.

The grim realities of trying to operate rice plantations with slave labor are revealed in documents of the Allston family of South Carolina, owners of large acreages in the Georgetown District watered by the Pee Dee and Waccamaw rivers. In 1840 the white population of the district was 2,193 with 18,274 slaves.

Various members of the family gradually acquired thousands of acres of tidal lands and became the largest rice growers in the region. Slaves on the plantations numbered from 25 or 30 to 200 and more; the numbers on each plantation varied as Allstons died and their legacies were divided or as they traded slaves among themselves; rarely did they sell slaves outside the family.

But rich as the Allstons were in land and slaves, life was difficult for them. The mere possession of human chattels was a burdensome responsibility, for slaves, which averaged about $750 each in price, had to be kept in good health or one lost on the investment, and in the swamp country the notion of African immunity to malaria proved a myth. Doctors were constantly being called to treat ailing servants, and not even the best of attention kept some of them from untimely death. Competent overseers were also hard to find and retain. Because the Allstons were humane planters, they would not put up with brutal overseers; even so, they could not prevent occasional incidents of cruelty, and more than one overseer was discharged for using the lash on Allston slaves.

Try as they could, discipline and competent direction of the field hands were difficult to maintain. Many of the laborers managed to shirk their tasks or to perform them incompetently. Plantation owners and their wives had to be constantly on the alert to supervise the labor of house servants, as well as field hands, to prevent costly mistakes and outright disasters. A canal gate carelessly left open might flood the fields at the wrong time. A quarrel among servants had to be adjudicated with the wisdom of Solomon to prevent feuds and fights. Illnesses and pretended illness had to be investigated and cared for.

Furthermore, life in the plantation house in the "sickly season"—from late May until early November—was less than pleasant. The climate was humid and hot, mosquitoes swarmed by the millions, and malaria was endemic. The planter and his family usually tried to retire to one of the sea islands or to the cooler pine barrens out of reach of "swamp fever." But the Allstons had to remain close enough to get back to their plantations once or twice a week to maintain proper supervision. Hard work rather than dainty dalliance was the lot of the average planter, even the wealthiest.

The Allstons believed that a planter ought to have a profession in addition to being a rice grower. One of the family, Washington Allston, even moved away to Cambridge, Massachusetts, and became a famous painter. Others were content with less exalted skills, but some became physicians, professional soldiers and engineers.

Robert Allston, son of Benjamin Allston, Jr., who died in 1809 leaving his plantations to the management of his long-suffering widow, Charlotte Ann, went to the Military Academy at West Point like others of his social class. His mother wrote to her son on April 2, 1821, saying that she had her debts in better shape, that his favorite slaves sent him greetings, that one, Joe, was riding a horse in the February races, that she was making him shirts, and that a supply of sweet potatoes was on the way to West Point: "Mr. Tucker sent you a barrel of sweet potatoes; they went down by Captain Toby to Charleston, but by whom they were shipped from thence I have not heard."[2] Robert graduated from the academy and for a time was on duty with the Topographical Service before returning to South Carolina to take his place among the aristocratic rice planters and to become, in 1856, governor of the state. Even in such families slaveowning and plantation management caused endless worry, perplexity, and trouble. Life for the planter at best was cursed, as it was for the chattels he owned.

Actually, slaveholders were a minority in the South, and thousands of Southerners never possessed a bondman. A historian, Kenneth M. Stamp, points out that "nearly three-fourths of all free Southerners had no connection with slavery through family ties or direct ownership. The 'typical' Southerner was not only a small farmer but also a non-slaveholder."[3] The nonslaveholders almost to a man were opposed to the system, which resulted in unfair competi-

150

tion. In South Carolina, for example, a few great planters with gangs of slaves monopolized the best lands in the tide-water region, but the up-country, as the piedmont area was designated, was peopled by a horde of small, independent farmers, many of them of Scotch-Irish and German descent. They were chiefly subsistence farmers, growing nearly everything they needed for daily use, with no help except that of their families. In times of harvest or house building, neighbors would join forces to help each other.

These farmers of the up-country raised large herds of cattle, which fattened on the wild pea vines and abundant grass of the region, for this rolling land was fertile. Probably the first cowboys in America were Scots living in the northwest corner of South Carolina. Their occupation is commemorated in the name of a village, Cowpens, site of a battle of the Revolutionary War where General Daniel Morgan soundly whipped the British under Bavastre Tarleton in January, 1781. The tough Scots cattlemen of upper South Carolina drove their livestock to the Charleston market and with the proceeds bought sugar, tea (and later coffee), guns, ammunition, utensils, and other commodities that the backcountry could not produce. These people had no use for slavery; their animosity toward the low-country aristocrats persisted for generations and remained a constant factor in South Carolina politics into the present century. Similar conditions prevailed in other Southern states. Before 1860, however, the great planters exercised the dominant political power.

Although cotton, rice, and sugarcane were the most profitable money crops in the South, they were by no means the only products of this agricultural region. The cattle raised in the upper South made an important contribution; at the present time the same region has given up cotton and has returned to cattle raising. The fame of Kentucky's race-horses spread throughout the nation, and the blue-grass country was soon dotted with horse pastures. Elsewhere in Kentucky and in Tennessee, Arkansas, and Missouri hemp

151

was a profitable crop. Its coarse fibers were woven into bagging used to wrap cotton bales, and some of its finer fibers were woven into cloth for slave clothing.

Agricultural developments in the West between 1830 and 1860 had enormous implications for the future of the United States. That region began to produce crops and livestock that would add to the riches of the nation, attract immigrants by the thousands, and have a great impact upon industry and life in the rest of the country.

The controversy over whether slavery would be permitted in new states west of the Mississippi had been temporarily quieted in 1820 by the celebrated Missouri Compromise, an act of Congress that admitted Missouri as a slave state but forbade slavery in any other portion of the United States north of Missouri's southern border, or latitude 36° 30'. That threw open huge areas of rich prairie lands to free settlers unwilling to migrate to any of the slave territories.

Pioneers from Europe and from the older sections of the United States poured into the Middle West after 1820. Conditions were different from the forest lands, where earlier settlers had to clear land of trees before they could plant a crop. On the flat or rolling prairies they had only to break the thick sod, plant seed, and hope for rain. After the first crop or two the primeval grass sod had rotted, and the land was more easily plowed. With favorable rains wheat, corn, and other grains flourished luxuriantly.

Unlike the forest lands to the east, the prairies provided little wood for fuel or building, and the pioneers had to contrive makeshift materials. Their first houses were built of blocks of sod and thatched with the same material. A piece of cowhide served to cover the doorway. Dried buffalo dung, called buffalo chips, found scattered over undisturbed portions of the prairie, could be used for fuel. A buffalo robe or a cowhide or two supplied the place of a plank floor.

Scarcity of water was often the prairie farmer's most

Converting the grassy prairies of the Midwest to farmland required improved plows pulled by teams of oxen to break up the heavy sod. Even with such equipment, it was hard work, and the men pictured here have paused to refresh themselves and the cattle. *Wood engraving in* Harper's Weekly, *August 10, 1867. Courtesy, Library of Congress.*

serious problem. He could scoop out a declivity and make what he called a tank to hold rainwater for his livestock. For drinking water he might dig a well where there was hope of striking underground water, or he had to haul water from a distant spring or stream. In any event life was laborious in the days before adequate transportation reached him.

But by 1840 railroads were sending their tentacles into the prairie region, and the northern portion of the Middle West was solving its transportation problems. Now lumber and hardware could reach the farmer and he could ship his grain and livestock to market. River, canal, and lake shipping had long served farmers in reach of these older means of transportation. By 1860 Chicago had become an important market and railroad center. Its stockyards and slaughterhouses were focal points for cattle raisers throughout the region. Only in 1971 did the stockyards of Chicago close because of the shift of meat-packing to less congested areas of the West.

An improvement in farm implements and the invention of laborsaving agricultural machinery helped revolutionize farming. Since the Middle Ages farm laborers had used spades, hoes, rakes, forks, and wooden plows. They had cut grain with a hand sickle and had threshed it with hand flails or by having oxen or horses walk around a threshing floor trampling out the grain. Even in colonial times agricultural technology had made few advances. Better plows were in use, it is true, but not yet had anyone thought of using detachable metal plow points that could be sharpened.

Because farmers are by nature conservative, technological improvements were slow. When Charles Newbold of New Jersey in 1797 patented a cast-iron plow, he had trouble persuading farmers to use it because some of them claimed that iron "poisoned the land." An improvement on Newbold's one-piece iron plow came in 1819, when a New Yorker invented a plow with detachable parts which could be bolted together. Gradually plows improved, farmers were converted to their use, and tough prairie sod could be turned more easily.

Almost as important as the improvement in plows was the invention of reaping and threshing machinery. A simple mowing machine preceded the development of the reaper. Practical reapers were independently invented by two men, Obed Hussey, who patented his machine in 1833, and Cyrus McCormick, who got a patent the following year. McCormick proved the better businessman, and McCormick reapers made a fortune for his family. Before 1860 more than 10,000 reapers, ideally suited to flat land, were operating on prairie farms.

Threshing machines came next. Using a hand flail to beat out the kernels, a man could thresh only eight to sixteen bushels of wheat in a day, which then had to be winnowed in the wind to separate the grain from the chaff. Power-operated threshing machines were invented independently in the United States and in England in the 1850's, but an American thresher developed by Hiram and John Pitts

154

Old and "new" methods of reaping compared: These two engravings from *Harper's Weekly* for August 1, 1857, illustrate the efficiency of the new McCormick reapers as against the older method of reaping and bundling the sheaves by hand. *Courtesy, Library of Congress.*

proved more efficient; one of their first machines, equipped with a winnowing fan, turned out more than twenty bushels of wheat an hour. These machines, rapidly improved, made threshing a much simpler process.

Threshing was an exciting occasion on any farm. The thresher was a huge, clumsy, red, boxlike machine, bigger than the largest wagon. Pulled by oxen or four mules, it was drawn into place near the stacked grain. An equally awkward steam engine with a tall smokestack covered by a spark arrester supplied the power. When the oxen had pulled the engine into place, discreetly positioned so the wind would not blow sparks into the straw, a fire was started in the firebox, leather belts were attached to the thresher, the feeders took their positions on the rear platform of the machine, the whistle blew, wheels began to turn, and the men began furiously to feed sheaves of grain into the machine's maw. The grain poured through a channel into sacks, and the straw and chaff blew into a pile on one side. It was hot and dusty work.

By noon everybody, tired and thirsty, quit for an enormous meal that the housewife, with the help of neighbors, had prepared. Thresher crews were a hungry lot, and farmers' wives spent days getting ready for the great day, which every child looked forward to for weeks. Modern combines which cut, thresh, and sack the grain as they go have robbed the farm of the most exciting day each year in a country boy's life.

Even the invention of laborsaving devices did not save the farmer and his family from hard work in any section of the United States. During the growing season his hours of labor were from dawn to dusk, for he had a constant battle against grass and weeds that would choke his crops. During the harvest season corn, grain, or hay had to be gathered before wind and rain ruined it. He was constantly at the mercy of the elements, and he watched the skies with the earnestness of a sailor trying to foretell the weather to come. Droughts, floods, wind, and hail could be his ruin. Most farmers became fatalists and made the best of misfor-

Threshing machines, invented in the 1850's, provided a time of excitement and sociability in the quiet routine of farm life. *Wood engraving in* Harper's, *September 21, 1878, after a sketch by O. D. Steinberger. Courtesy, Library of Congress.*

tune when it came. The pious said, "It is the will of God"; the less Christian swore and grumbled but resolutely turned to repair the damage as best they could and plant another crop.

In many sections the late summer was called the lay-by season. For by that time the crops were well grown, the battle against grass and weeds was won, and the farmer had merely to wait for his corn, cotton, or other summer crops to mature; for a few weeks his crops were laid by. Then he could go fishing, visit with neighbors, attend religious revivals and camp meetings, listen to candidates for office speaking at the county courthouse, and take what recreation pleased him best.

During the lay-by season farmers gathered at crossroad stores and swapped yarns. They became adept at telling tall stories, for the exaggerated tale was characteristic of the countryman's humor. For example, in the West farmers liked to emphasize the richness of the soil. One story reported that watermelon vines grew so fast in the Brazos Valley that no melons ever got big enough to ripen. The reason: The fast-moving vines wore the little melons out dragging them along the ground before they had time to mature. Farmers liked to match wits in what they called a liars' contest, and their tall tales became a part of country folklore.

Yet even in the lay-by or winter season, a farmer's work was never done. Today he can drive his tractor under a shed and leave it until spring if need be. But in pretractor days he had horses, mules, and oxen to feed and water. Always there were cows to milk, morning and night. Sometimes this was the farm wife's chore; sometimes the boys and girls of the family did the milking. Then there was the problem of taking care of the milk and churning the cream into butter.

The poultry also required constant care. Before the days of incubators and day-old chicks bought from commercial hatcheries, broody hens had to be set with a dozen to fifteen eggs and watched for three weeks until the eggs hatched. Such a hen—in defiance of grammar—was always a "setting," never a sitting, hen. Baby chicks had to be herded under shelter at the approach of thunderstorms because heavy rains would drown them. Turkey raising was even more trouble, for young turkeys had a fatal impulse to drown; if caught in the open during a downpour, they would turn their heads to heaven and die.

Although their life was full of hardships and frustrations, farmers were hardy, independent, and self-reliant. They had not yet learned that a beneficent government might bail them out of difficulties. They might grumble in plenty, but they contrived to survive and frequently to prosper.

Chapter 9

The Lure of the Sea

From colonial days to the beginning of the Civil War careers at sea attracted thousands of young men, especially New Englanders. In that region for many families "going to sea" was traditional. From earliest times fishing had been one of New England's important industries, and the fisheries proved the nursery of blue-water sailors. Nantucket and Long Island specialized in whaling, at first in their own coastal waters and later, as whales grew scarcer, in distant seas. Frequently their crews included Indians skillful in throwing harpoons. Not only did New England build great numbers of ships, but it supplied much of the manpower for their navigation. By the end of the Revolution ships manned by American seamen were probing the seven seas.

Before the Revolution fishing for cod and mackerel had made many New England families prosperous. Ships went out from Boston, Gloucester, Salem, and numerous other New England towns as far as the Grand Banks off New-foundland in search of cod. There the fish were cleaned, split open, salted, and dried on wooden racks ashore. Then they were barreled for shipment to Mediterranean coun-

159

In the early days of the nation, before the large-scale development of industry or of mass transportation, seafaring was perhaps the most glamorous—and crowded—career open to adventurous young men. It has been estimated that 40,000 sailors put to sea from New England ports during the heyday of the whaling industry. The opportunity to "see the world," however, was paid for in prolonged absences from home; whaling voyages often took three years or more. *Currier lithograph, 1847. Courtesy, Library of Congress.*

tries, where they were in demand. Mackerel, caught in great quantities off the North Atlantic coast, were dried or pickled in brine for shipment to the West Indies, where sugar planters required large quantities of fish for their slave workers. After the Revolution the British placed restrictions on the shipment of dried fish to their islands of the West Indies, but in time New England fishermen contrived either to evade the law or to find other markets. Fishing remained an important enterprise.

American shippers even before the Revolution had found means of getting around Britain's efforts to curb colonial enterprise on the high seas. For example, after Parliament passed the Molasses Act of 1733 placing a tax of sixpence a gallon on molasses obtained from non-British sources, smuggling became almost an act of virtue. Lessons learned earlier in the evasion of restrictive laws stood New England shippers in good stead after achieving independence. Although much uncertainty about trade existed for the next decade, Yankee ships continued to ply the seas and turn a profit.

Faced with British efforts to curtail trade with the West Indies, merchants in the new nation sought other sources of revenue. For generations the East India Company had supplied Oriental products to England and its colonies. The tea that the Boston Tea Party tossed into the bay, for example, was a shipment from the East India Company. Why not cut into this lucrative trade, reasoned farsighted merchants in Boston, Salem, Providence, New York, and Philadelphia. It would make up for the loss of business with West Indian markets. Consequently, in February, 1784, a New York firm dispatched to Canton a vessel aptly named the *Empress of China*. After a year and three months this ship docked again in New York with a valuable cargo of silk, tea, and Chinese knickknacks, bought with American silver, for as yet the Chinese showed little interest in American products. Thus began the China trade. But even a one-way trade of this sort proved profitable, and it was not unusual for the early voyages to China to return a profit of 100 percent or more.

Soon American ships were swarming to the Far East. The first American vessel in the Philippines was the *Astrea*, sent out in 1796 by a Salem merchant. Other Salem ships quickly followed to the Spice Islands of Indonesia and to other strange ports around the world. By 1788 nearly fifty ships had cleared for Far Eastern ports. One Salem skipper brought back from Sumatra a cargo of pepper that realized a profit of 800 percent. It was small wonder that tales of

The harbor of Canton, China, in the first half of the nineteenth century, with international trading areas marked by the flags of nations with commercial treaties.

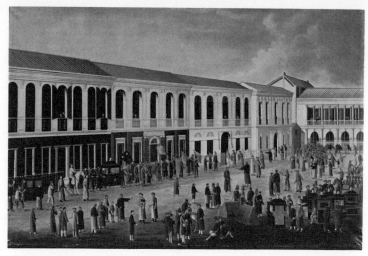

A close-up of the Canton port area, with the houses of international trade in the background. Note the "parking lot" for sedan chairs of Cantonese merchants at lower right and the Western dress of foreign agents looking out of the windows. *Both are paintings preserved in the Henry Francis du Pont Winterthur Museum. Photographs, courtesy of the museum.*

exotic lands and great rewards stirred prosaic merchants to exert themselves in the new trade until American seamen were a common sight swaggering along eastern waterfronts from Manila to Canton. The stories they brought back excited youths in droves to sign on for voyages that might take as long as three years or more before they saw their home ports again.

A seaman on an East Indian voyage, whether by way of Cape Horn or the Cape of Good Hope, could be certain of rugged adventure. Weather off either cape was normally rough. But weather was not the only hazard. The islands of the East Indies swarmed with pirates ready to board a carelessly guarded vessel, rob and scuttle it, and send all hands to the bottom. More than one American craft fell victim to Indonesian pirates.

American merchants trading to China were troubled because they had to pay for Chinese wares in cash rather than by the exchange of products. At first the only commodity that attracted much Chinese interest was an herb, ginseng, which grew in many parts of the United States. Chinese herb doctors, then as now, regarded it as a cure for a variety of diseases and a restorative of vigor to old men. In the colonial period William Byrd of Virginia had also recommended ginseng for sundry ailments. To procure ginseng for the China trade, New England merchants sent boys, girls, and woodsmen searching the uplands for the roots of this plant. For a time it helped in the balance of payments with China, but the market was soon glutted. Not even all China could use up the amount of ginseng that diligent search of American woods produced.

After various experiments American traders discovered a more valuable commodity for the Chinese market. Someone heard that furs, particularly the smooth glossy skins of sea otters from the Pacific Northwest, were much in demand in Canton. The first Americans to experiment with this traffic were two sea captains from Boston, Robert Gray and John Kendrick. Bound around the Horn for Nootka Sound in British Columbia, they sailed from Boston early in 1787, Kendrick in command of the *Columbia* and Gray in command of the *Washington* (sometimes referred to as the *Lady Washington*).

After reaching their destination and getting a cargo of furs in exchange for hatchets, other hardware, and trinkets, Kendrick transferred command of the *Columbia* to Gray, who sailed on July 30, 1789, for Canton. Selling his furs and loading silk and tea, he weighed anchor for his home port, sailing by way of the Cape of Good Hope, and

Much "Chinese export" porcelain and stoneware was made to order. Most famous of these was President Washington's, whose 306-piece dinner set in blue-and-white Fitzhugh was decorated with the eagle of the Society of the Cincinnati. Shown here is the soup tureen of this set. Courtesy, *The Henry Francis du Pont Winterthur Museum.*

reached Boston on August 10, 1790, the first American to carry the new flag around the world. He had traveled more than 42,000 miles. Boston gave him a hero's welcome, but Gray was not a man to rest on his laurels. In September he had the *Columbia* shipshape, a crew recruited, and was ready again to duplicate his previous voyage.

On Gray's second journey he reached Vancouver Island in June, 1791. By the following spring he had a cargo of sea otter skins and was ready to sail for China once more. But this time he made an important discovery. Pushing his ship through a line of breakers, he rode into the mouth of a great river which he named the Columbia after his ship. His discovery of the Columbia River helped establish the United States' claim to the Oregon territory. Gray went on to China, sold his furs, obtained the usual freight of Chinese goods, and reached Boston on July 20, 1793. A three years' voyage was not unusual in this trade.

One of Gray's seamen observed that the mouth of the Columbia River would be a good place for a trading post. There in 1810 John Jacob Astor established Astoria, western headquarters of his American Fur Company; he hoped for a lucrative trade in furs with China, but unhappily for him the War of 1812 forced his resident factor to sell out to a British firm, the Northwest Company, just ahead of Astoria's capture by a man-of-war.

After Gray's departure for Canton on his first voyage Captain Kendrick remained in the Northwest for a time, trading with the Indians, building a small fort, and negotiating for land. He then turned the *Washington*'s prow toward China but dallied in Hawaii (then called the Sandwich Islands) trying to arrange for a trade in pearls and sandalwood. He finally reached China in 1791 but decided to return to the Northwest by way of Japan to investigate the possibilities of a Japanese market for furs. Kendrick was the first American to fly the flag in Japan. Finding the Japanese disinterested, he continued his trading ventures between China, the Northwest, and Hawaii. In Hawaii in 1794 he took a successful part in an intertribal conflict but shortly thereafter was accidentally killed by a cannonball fired by a captain attempting to give him a salute. Such was the life and death of one Yankee adventurer in the Pacific.

American trade with the Far East, especially with China, not only brought immense profits to merchants engaged in it, but influenced American taste in several respects. American tables were soon supplied with Chinese porcelain and pottery; American women could buy silks, laces, and embroideries at lower prices; Chinese Chippendale furniture became popular; Chinese firecrackers, sold in small red bunches, crackled on the Fourth of July; and even Chinese herb remedies and nostrums (reciprocity for ginseng, perhaps) found their way to the apothecaries. Before the middle of the century medicine vendors and proprietors of medicine shows were capitalizing upon Oriental interest by offering Dr. Lin's Celestial Balm of China, capable of relieving any ache or bruise; Dr. Drake's Canton Chinese Hair Cream, a positive cure for baldness; and countless restoratives to make "old men young and young men younger."[1] Interest in China clearly was not confined to the captains and sailors who strode about the wharfs of Canton.

Yankee traders in China had to learn the ways of the East if they hoped to succeed. Business, which could not be hurried, had to be conducted with ceremony to which sea captains were unaccustomed. And everywhere money had to be laid out for graft and gratuities called cumshaw. The diaries and logbooks of captains in the China trade are filled with grumblings about the amount of graft required, but this was the custom, and nothing could change it. In much of the Far East the custom has not yet changed.

Trade with the Chinese suffered a setback in the mid-century as a result of a civil war known as the Taiping Rebellion, which broke out in 1850. Interest in the possibility of American trade with Japan, previously closed to all except a few Dutch and Chinese merchants, had been growing; the curtailment of commerce with China

165

stimulated efforts to open Japan to American ships. To that end President Millard Fillmore in 1853 sent a naval squadron commanded by Commodore Matthew Calbraith Perry to make a bold demand for American rights of trade. Perry sailed into Tokyo Bay and cast anchor on July 8, 1853. Two of his vessels, the *Mississippi* and the *Susquehanna*, were powered by steam, and these alone created a sensation. Perry delivered a message for the emperor to port officials and departed while the Japanese debated the matter. In February, 1854, he returned with a panoply of gifts for the Japanese in case of a favorable decision and heavy armament in case he might need to use force. Luckily the progressive Japanese had persuaded the emperor and the shogun (the real power at the moment) that trade would be beneficial, and thus Japan was opened to American commerce. Perry delivered his gifts at Yokohama; they included a model locomotive, a copy of Audubon's *Birds of America*, and a barrel of whiskey. Perhaps the Japanese liking for American bourbon can be dated from the consumption of this barrel.

The Far Eastern trade provided an opportunity for American seamen to experience exotic pleasures in Hawaii, the usual point of refreshment on every voyage. After collecting furs along the damp and foggy shores of the Pacific Northwest, ships ordinarily made for the sunny Sandwich Islands, where they might refit, take on fruits and vegetables, and give the sailors a time for rest and recreation before proceeding across the Pacific. In many cases they wintered in the islands, which appeared a paradise to some, but to others of the more puritanical kind they were the devil's domain. To a lad brought up in the strict Puritanism of Salem or Gloucester, the sight of nude Polynesian maidens swimming out to welcome the seamen gave a jolt to his emotions that blunted the recollections of sermons threatening hellfire to those who succumbed to concupiscence.

The whaling and sealing industry in the first half of the

nineteenth century gave American seamen preeminence in distant oceans and made them the discoverers of many islands in the South Seas. Americans in pursuit of fur seals and whales, there is reason to believe, may have been the first to discover land in the Antarctic. Logbooks kept by whalers between 1820 and 1850 provided data about many half-forgotten islands that the United States Navy found useful during World War II. Indeed, in some cases soundings and charts made by these early navigators supplied the best information available to our Navy in 1942. For whaling captains and seal hunters pushed their vessels into every corner of the South Pacific. In some cases they smashed their ships on hidden coral reefs; a few fell victims to islanders who swarmed aboard and murdered crews; others were lured ashore and slaughtered to provide "long pig" for cannibal feasts; others, however, were given such a welcome to idyllic spots in the South Seas that sailors occasionally refused to leave. Later shipwrecked seamen sometimes found on isolated islands white Americans who had "gone native" and were living contentedly under waving coconut palms.

A harpooner poised to strike as a whaleboat comes alongside one of the giant mammals. In the background a previous catch is being stripped of blubber and the try-pots are already smoking. *Lithograph by Currier & Ives (n.d.). Courtesy, Library of Congress.*

A close-up of the process of "cutting in." Strips of blubber were cut off in a spiral, like peeling an orange, as the whale carcass slowly rotated. Sharks in the foreground have gathered for a feast. *Engraving in Ballou's Pictorial, February 17, 1855, after a drawing by Wade. Courtesy, Eleutherian Mills Historical Library.*

Between 1820 and 1830 Americans gained world supremacy in whaling, and by 1846 the total American whaling fleet, counting oceangoing craft of all types, amounted to 735 vessels. The whole whaling fleet of foreigners totaled only 230 vessels. Early in the nineteenth century some whalers transferred to English and French bases and sailed under those respective flags to avoid English and French taxes on whale oil. For many years both English and French whaling ships frequently employed Nantucket captains, who brought along a few of their countrymen to serve in the crews.

Whaling drew large numbers of boys from the farms of New England; some enlisted when they were very young; before he was out of his teens, many a boy was already a skillful harpooner (or boat steerer, as he was called at the time, for he had dual duties). After the movement to the West gained momentum, especially after the gold rush to

168

California, the recruitment of farm boys was harder, and whaling ships had to take more riffraff off the streets of port towns. The quality of their crews noticeably deteriorated in these later years, and life in the forecastle (living quarters of the crew) was tougher.

Whaling might sound like one long series of thrilling adventures as a ship's recruiter talked to a Vermont farm boy, but the youth found conditions different once he was aboard and out of sight of land. Even the stoutest wooden ship must have seemed to a boy fresh from the farm a frail refuge from the threats of wind and waves. Furthermore, the old salts aboard unmercifully hazed the "greenie," as the new recruit was called, and they scared the daylights out of him with tales of ships sunk by rogue whales ramming them head on or with stories about cannibals boarding vessels in the South Seas and slaughtering whole crews for dinner. To sailors before the mast all natives of the Pacific islands were cannibals, though actually cannibalism was rare.

A new recruit on a whaling ship had to learn seamanship and the particular techniques of whaling. For example, he had to take his turn in the crow's nest as lookout for these sea monsters and to call out "Thar she blows!" when one was seen. On sighting a whale two and sometimes three boats were lowered from the davits, and the recruit took his place at the oars as they pulled away in pursuit of the quarry. Once alongside, the harpooner drove his iron into the beast as close as possible to the back of his head and the excitement began. Attached to the harpoon was a thin rope more than a thousand yards long coiled in a tub. After being struck, the whale either sounded (dived) or took off, towing the boat at a dizzying speed for what whalers called a Nantucket sleigh ride. Sometimes the rope payed out so fast that someone had to slosh water on the line to prevent its burning through from friction. If all went well, the whale either came to the surface or stopped from exhaustion; the lancers could then finish the kill.

169

The creature next had to be towed back to the ship and lashed alongside. With long-handled implements like spades, sharp as razors, the seamen cut into the body and stripped it of blubber (fat), which was hoisted up in tubs. On a deck covered with brick and equipped with furnaces and pots the blubber was tried out (melted into liquid). Fire under the pots, started with wood, was later fueled with the crisp scraps from the melted blubber. Black smoke spread soot over everything, and the stench permeated the whole ship. Oil-soaked decks were an ever-present fire hazard but, oddly, few ships appear to have been destroyed by fire.

The best oil, known as spermaceti, came from the heads of a species called sperm whales. Spermaceti burned with the clearest light in oil lamps and made the best candles; hence it brought the best price, and sperm whales were the ones most sought. Spermaceti was found in a natural container, called the case, in the sperm whale's head; this case was frequently as much as two feet across and six feet deep. Consequently, while some of the workers were stripping blubber for the cruder oil, others cut off the sperm whale's enormous head, half hoisted it to the deck, and dipped out the spermaceti. Of the several species of whale hunted for their oil, the much-sought sperm whale was the most dangerous to whalemen.

From the mouth of another species, the Greenland or right whale, came flexible strips used to strengthen women's corsets. This whalebone, technically called baleen, which among other uses supplied ribs for umbrellas, was much in demand before thin steel strips supplanted it. Whalebone came from an intricate system of strainers in the back of the whale's mouth which enabled it to winnow out plankton and other small foodstuffs from seawater.

Not always was the whaler lucky enough to make a kill without disaster, for whales sometimes turned on the boats and crushed them in their jaws, dived under and capsized them, or smashed them with tail or flukes. Forecastle yarns of boat-destroying whales were endless. In a few substantiated instances whales even sank the mother ships as well.

One such instance was the fate of the Nantucket whaler *Essex*, Captain George Pollard commanding, which on November 20, 1820, somewhere below the equator between the Galápagos Islands and the Marquesas, was rammed by an angry eighty-five-foot sperm whale, stove in, and sunk. The first mate, Owen Chase, saw the whale heading toward the vessel and ordered the helmsman to sheer off but, as he stated, "The words were scarcely out of my mouth before he came down upon us with full speed and struck the ship with his head, just forward of the fore chains. He gave us such an appalling and tremendous jar as nearly threw us on our faces. The ship brought up . . . violently as if she had struck a rock and trembled for a few minutes like a leaf."[2] Not content with ramming the *Essex* once, the whale turned and made a second attack, which stove in the whole bow section. In a few minutes the *Essex* was a sinking wreck.

The crew of twenty in three open boats set out from mid-Pacific for the coast of South America. They had salvaged some food, water, two quadrants, and two compasses from the wreck; with this meager equipment they hoped to reach Chile or Peru. On December 20 they sighted a barren and uninhabited bit of land, now called Henderson Island. A tiny spring, a few birds, and a little pepper grass gave its only hope of sustenance, but three of the crew elected to stay there instead of going on when the boats pushed off. On January 12 a storm separated First Mate Chase's boat from the others; nearly three weeks later a second boat disappeared in a heavy sea; that left Chase's and Captain Pollard's boats afloat but out of sight of each other.

In both boats men died, and the awful decision was made to eat their remains. At last, when only four men were left in the captain's boat and they were nearing starvation again, they agreed to cast lots to see who would be killed to provide food for the rest. The lot fell on the captain's nephew, Owen Coffin. Though the captain offered to take his place, Coffin insisted on being the sacrifice, bowed his head, and was killed by Seaman Charles Ramsdell, who had drawn the lot to be executioner. That left three alive. Soon another man died, and Pollard and Ramsdell lived on the remains until picked up on February 23, more dead than alive, in sight of land, by a Nantucket whaleship, the *Dauphin*, Captain Zimri Coffin. In the meantime Owen Chase, the first mate, with two other survivors, had been picked up by the London whaler *Indian*, Captain William Crozier. The five men rescued from the two boats finally were reunited in Valparaiso, where they told their story to the commander of the United States frigate *Constellation*, then in port. He paid an English skipper bound for Australia $300 to go by way of Henderson Island and pick up the three marooned sailors there, which he did. Thus eight of the twenty aboard the *Essex* lived to tell a tale that was repeated in forecastles as long as whalers continued to sail the seas.

Owen Chase wrote an account of the episode, published in 1821 as the *Narrative of the Most Extraordinary and Distressing Shipwreck of the Whaleship Essex of Nantucket*. This was read by Herman Melville and supplied suggestions for his novel *Moby Dick*, published in 1851. Melville himself in January, 1841, had sailed out of New Bedford (which succeeded Nantucket as the nation's chief whaling port) as a foremast hand aboard the whaler *Acushnet*. With a companion, Richard Tobias Greene, Melville in July, 1842, jumped ship in the Marquesas, where the two lived with natives of the interior until they decided to escape on an Australian trading schooner. Melville deserted again in Tahiti; at length, after serving on another whaler long enough to get to Honolulu, he shipped aboard the American ship of war *United States*, from which he was mustered out in Boston in September, 1842.

This was the career of one young American, not unlike that of many others, except that this one used his experiences as material for books that have given him immortality as a writer. His first autobiographical novel, *Typee*, published in 1846, described his life among the Marquesans with a romantic picture of the beautiful maiden Fayal. Many a youthful reader must have yearned to follow in Melville's footsteps, even at the risk of the cannibals whom he also described. Although *Moby Dick*, Melville's greatest novel, is filled with symbolism of man's struggle with evil in the world, it has many realistic passages describing life at sea and the whole business of whaling.

Melville got his idea for the great white whale Moby Dick from forecastle yarns about a terrible sperm whale called Mocha Dick, so named because he was first sighted off the island of Mocha on the Chilean coast. During the 1830's and '40's a number of ships reported encounters with the monster. In July, 1840, the English whaler *Desmond* off Valparaiso had two of its boats crushed in the jaws of a monstrous gray whale and lost two seamen in the wreckage. A month later a Russian whaler lost a boat to Mocha Dick. In May, 1841, the crew of the Bristol whaler *John Day* attacked Mocha Dick east of the Falkland Islands not far from Cape Horn. Although they got a harpoon in the whale, it got away after smashing two boats and killing two men. In October, 1842, Mocha Dick rammed and sank a small lumber schooner off the Japanese coast. Three whaling ships in the area rescued the sailors and set out to hunt down the monster. Again the whale smashed boats, crushed sailors in its jaws, and left the sea littered with wreckage and bleeding men before disappearing.

An account of Mocha Dick is given in detail in A. B. C. Whipple's *Yankee Whalers in the South Seas*. Whipple comments: "Could this white or off-white whale be the same one in each encounter—striking first in mid-Pacific, then in the South Atlantic, then off the coast of Japan? Probably not. But forecastle legend maintained that it was."[3] At any rate, the story of the monster, widely circulated in maritime circles, lent realism to Melville's novel.

Other vessels encountered ferocious whales and lost boats and men in the attacks. In 1850 the *Pocahontas* was rammed by a whale off the Brazilian coast and barely limped into Rio de Janeiro. A year later a New Bedford whaler, the *Ann Alexander*, Captain John S. Deblois, harpooned a whale in the Pacific but lost two boats when the beast charged with open jaws and crushed them to bits. Angry and determined, Captain Deblois tried to run the whale down with this ship, a decision that proved a mistake. Just at dusk the whale charged at terrific speed, hitting the *Ann Alexander* forward of the mainmast, smashing a gaping hole, and leaving her a wreck. Luckily ships in the vicinity rescued the crew. Five months later another New Bedford crew killed a sickly whale with a head full of splinters. It had in it harpoons from the *Ann Alexander*. Thus the New Bedford men were avenged.

Whales were not the only game that ships sought in the great oceans. In the same period some ships went after seals wherever they could find them, even to the very edge of the Antarctic continent. They were more secretive than the whalers because they did not want others to discover the sources of their furs. Theirs was hard and bloody work, for they had to go ashore, club the seals to death, skin them, salt their hides, and load them into the holds. The smell aboard a sealer full of stinking hides was even worse than that on a whaler. The men were more taciturn and less given to communication with other ships at sea.

Whalers, on the other hand, were eager to "speak" to one another when they met in the open sea. They would usually heave to, the captains would meet on one or the other ship, and the crews would exchange visits. For a day or two they would have what they called a gam—a gabfest—while they swapped experiences, retold yarns long familiar to seamen, and tried to outdo each other with tales of pretty girls on moonlit beaches in the South Seas.

But soon they would up anchors and be on their way into the lonely reaches of the ocean again. A whaling ship might pass days, weeks, even months, of tedious cruising without

Clippers in the California trade and ships of all kinds bringing passengers to the gold fields crowded the harbor of San Francisco at midcentury. This view from Telegraph Hill was drawn by William B. McMurtrie, draftsman attached to a U.S. surveying expedition, in April, 1850. *Lithograph by N. Currier, 1851, after McMurtrie's drawing. Courtesy, Library of Congress.*

sighting a whale. To while away long, dull days, seamen carved designs on whale teeth (which were always given the crews after a kill). Sometimes these designs were pictures of ships, girls, or imagined landscapes, scratched into the surface and darkened with soot. This folk art came to be known as scrimshaw. Museums today have many examples of scrimshaw work, some showing great artistic skill. From larger pieces of bone sailors carved utilitarian objects such as rolling pins and even put together bird cages of bone. Occasionally whalers in the Pacific would stop at the Galápagos Islands to catch a few land turtles prized as food—and to pick up mail. For they had an informal post office there: a box into which a Nantucket, New Bedford, or other ship recently out of port would deposit mail addressed to someone on a vessel already in the Pacific. Sometimes the recipients got the messages, sometimes not. But it was at least worth a stop for a ship cruising in the region.

Some American ships began trading with California before the gold rush, for the ranchers in that region had vast herds of cattle that produced hides and tallow, needed for leather and candles in the United States. Not every American could afford clear-burning spermaceti candles and whale-oil lamps. Many still had to be content with tallow candles, and the West Coast was a good source of tallow.

175

One of the most fascinating accounts of this traffic was written by a Harvard student named Richard Henry Dana, Jr., who had been suspended from college in 1832 for participating in a student riot. The next year he contracted measles that affected his eyes so that he could not return to college. To improve his health, he shipped out of Boston in August, 1834, as an ordinary seaman aboard the brig *Pilgrim*, bound for California. On January 14, 1835, "after a voyage," Dana wrote, "of one hundred and fifty days from Boston," they reached Santa Barbara, their destination. In May he was sent ashore at San Diego to help in the curing of hides, and for several months he had an opportunity to observe life in California in these pre-American days. Finally, in May, 1836, he shipped in the *Alert* for Boston. Dana's *Two Years Before the Mast*, published anonymously in 1840, provides an unvarnished and graphic description of life at sea. His indignation at the cruelty of harsh sea captains and his efforts in behalf of seamen ultimately resulted in the passage of remedial laws.

Although a seaman's life was hard, whether aboard a trading ship, a whaler, or a sealer, the sea never lost its power to attract adventurous youths. It has always had a hypnotic attraction for many, and that attraction has not yet disappeared, even with the coming of jet aircraft that circumnavigate the globe in a matter of hours. Even 36,000 feet above the water, one is forever aware of the sea, and passengers watch from aircraft windows for a glimpse of something in the mystery below.

Why Men Go to Sea

Herman Melville, in the opening chapter of *Moby Dick* (1851), explains the irresistible pull of the sea.

Now when I say that I am in the habit of going to sea whenever I begin to grow hazy about the eyes and begin to be over-conscious of my lungs, I do not mean

to have it inferred that I ever go to sea as a passenger.
. . . No, when I go to sea I go as a simple sailor, right
before the mast, plumb down into the forecastle, aloft
there to the royal masthead. True, they rather order
me about some, and make me jump from spar to spar
like a grasshopper in a May meadow. And at first this
sort of thing is unpleasant enough. It touches one's
sense of honor, particularly if you come of an old established family in the land, the Van Rensselaers, or
Randolphs, or Hardicanutes. And more than all if just
previous to putting your hand into the tar pot you
have been lording it as a country schoolmaster, making the tallest boys stand in awe of you. The transition
is a keen one, I assure you, from a schoolmaster to a
sailor, and requires a strong decoction of Seneca and
the Stoics to enable you to grin and bear it. But even
this wears off in time.

What of it if some old hunks of a sea captain orders
me to get a broom and sweep down the decks? . . .
Who ain't a slave? Tell me that. Well then, however
the old sea captains may order me about—however
they may thump and punch me about—I have the satisfaction of knowing that it is all right; that everybody
else is one way or other served in much the same way
—either in a physical or metaphysical point of view,
that is. And so the universal thump is passed round,
and all hands should rub each other's shoulder blades
and be content.

Again, I always go to sea as a sailor because they
make a point of paying me for my trouble, whereas
they never pay passengers a single penny that I ever
heard of. On the contrary, passengers themselves must
pay. And there is all the difference in the world between paying and being paid. . . .

Finally, I always go to sea as a sailor because of the
wholesome exercise and pure air of the forecastle
deck. For, as in this world head winds are far more

prevalent than winds from astern . . . , so for the most part the Commodore on the quarter-deck gets his atmosphere at second hand from the sailors on the forecastle. He thinks he breathes it first; but not so. In much the same way do the commonalty lead their leaders in many other things, at the same time that the leaders little suspect it. But wherefore it was that, after having repeatedly smelt the sea as a merchant sailor, I should now take it into my head to go on a whaling voyage: this the invisible police officer of the Fates—who has the constant surveillance of me and secretly dogs me and influences me in some unaccountable way—he can better answer than anyone else. . . .

The *Pequod*'s Crew Kill a Sperm Whale

Melville in *Moby Dick* gives a vivid description of the whale hunt and all things connected with it. A few excerpts follow.

Close under our lee, not forty fathoms off, a gigantic sperm whale lay rolling in the water like the capsized hull of a frigate, his broad glossy back, of an Ethiopian hue, glistening in the sun's rays like a mirror. But lazily undulating in the trough of the sea, and ever and anon tranquilly spouting his vapory jet, the whale looked like a portly burgher smoking his pipe of a warm afternoon. . . .

"Clear away the boats! Luff!" cried Ahab. And, obeying his own order, he dashed the helm down before the helmsman could handle the spokes.

The sudden exclamations of the crew must have alarmed the whale, and, ere the boats were down, majestically turning, he swam away to the leeward, but with such a steady tranquillity and making so few ripples as he swam that, thinking after all he might not as yet be alarmed, Ahab gave orders that not an oar should be used, and no man must speak but in whispers. So, seated like Ontario Indians on the gunwales of the boats, we swiftly but silently paddled along; the calm not admitting of the noiseless sails being set. Presently, as we thus glided in chase, the monster perpendicularly flitted his tail forty feet into the air and then sank out of sight like a tower swallowed up.

"There go flukes!" was the cry, an announcement immediately followed by Stubb's producing his match and igniting his pipe, for now a respite was granted. After the full interval of his sounding had elapsed, the whale rose again and, being now in advance of the smoker's boat and much nearer to it than to any of the others, Stubb counted upon the honor of the capture. It was obvious, now, that the whale had at length become aware of his pursuers. All silence of cautiousness was therefore no longer of use. Paddles were dropped and oars came loudly into play. And still puffing at his pipe, Stubb cheered on his crew to the assault.

Yes, a mighty change had come over the fish. All alive to his jeopardy, he was going "head out," that part obliquely projecting from the mad yeast which he brewed.

"Start her, start her, my men! Don't hurry yourselves; take plenty of time—but start her; start her like thunderclaps, that's all," cried Stubb, spluttering out the smoke as he spoke. "Start her now; give 'em the long and strong stroke, Tashtego. Start her, Tash, my boy—start her, all; but keep cool, keep cool—cucumbers is the word—easy, easy—only start her like grim death and grinning devils, and raise the buried dead perpendicular out of their graves, boys—that's all. Start her!" . . .

"Ka-la! Koo-loo!" howled Queequeg, as if smacking his lips over a mouthful of Grenadier's steak. And thus

179

with oars and yells the keels cut the sea. Meanwhile Stubb, retaining his place in the van, still encouraged his men to the onset, all the while puffing the smoke from his mouth. Like desperadoes they tugged and they strained, till the welcome cry was heard: "Stand up, Tashtego! Give it to him!" The harpoon was hurled. "Stern all!" The oarsmen backed water; the same moment something went hot and hissing along every one of their wrists. It was the magical line. An instant before Stubb had swiftly caught two additional turns with it round the loggerhead, whence, by reason of its increased rapid circlings, a hempen blue smoke now jetted up and mingled with the steady fumes from his pipe. As the line passed round and round the log-gerhead, so also, just before reaching that point, it blisteringly passed through and through both of Stubb's hands, from which the hand-cloths, or squares of quilted canvas sometimes worn at these times, had accidentally dropped. It was like holding an enemy's sharp two-edged sword by the blade, and that enemy all the time striving to wrest it out of your clutch.

"Wet the line! Wet the line!" cried Stubb to the tub oarsman (him seated by the tub) who, snatching off his hat, dashed the sea-water into it. More turns were taken, so that the line began holding its place. The boat now flew through the boiling water like a shark all fins. Stubb and Tashtego here changed places —stem for stern—a staggering business truly in that rocking commotion. . . .

Thus they rushed, each man with might and main clinging to his seat to prevent being tossed to the foam; and the tall form of Tashtego at the steering oar crouching almost double in order to bring down his centre of gravity. Whole Atlantics and Pacifics seemed passed as they shot on their way, till at length the whale somewhat slackened his flight.

180

"Haul in, haul in!" cried Stubb to the bowsman. And, facing round toward the whale, all hands began pulling the boat up to him, while yet the boat was being towed on. Soon ranging up by his flank, Stubb, firmly planting his knee in the clumsy cleat, darted dart after dart into the flying fish; at the word of command the boat alternately sterning out of the way of the whale's horrible wallow and then ranging up for another fling.

The red tide now poured from all sides of the monster like brooks down a hill. His tormented body rolled not in brine but in blood, which bubbled and seethed for furlongs behind in their wake. The slanting sun playing upon this crimson pond in the sea sent back its reflection into every face, so that they all glowed to each other like red men. And all the while jet after jet of white smoke was agonizingly shot from the spiracle [blowhole] of the whale, and vehement puff after puff from the mouth of the excited headsman as at every dart, hauling in upon his crooked lance (by the line attached to it), Stubb straightened it again and again by a few rapid blows against the gunwale then again and again sent it into the whale.

"Pull up, pull up!' he now cried to the bowsman as the waning whale relaxed in his wrath. "Pull up! Close to!" and the boat ranged along the fish's flank. . . . And now it is struck. For, starting from his trance into that unspeakable thing called his "flurry," the monster horribly wallowed in his blood, overwrapped himself in impenetrable, mad, boiling spray so that the imperilled craft, instantly dropping astern, had much ado blindly to struggle out from that frenzied twilight into the clear air of the day.

And now, abating in his flurry, the whale once more rolled out into view, surging from side to side, spasmodically dilating and contracting his spout hole with sharp, cracking, agonized respirations. At last gush

181

after gush of clotted red gore, as if it had been the purple lees of red wine, shot into the frighted air and, falling back again, ran dripping down his motionless flanks into the sea. His heart had burst!

"He's dead, Mr. Stubb," said Daggoo.

Life at Sea

In *Two Years Before the Mast* Richard Henry Dana describes in detail the hardships and routine of life at sea. A few excerpts follow.

Wednesday, November 5th [1834] . . . Just before eight o'clock (then about sundown, in that latitude) the cry of "All hands ahoy!" was sounded down the fore scuttle and the after hatchway, and, hurrying upon deck, we found a large black cloud rolling on toward us from the southwest and darkening the whole heavens. "Here comes Cape Horn!" said the chief mate. And we had hardly time to haul down and clew up before it was upon us. In a few minutes a heavier sea was raised than I had ever seen, and, as it was directly ahead, the little brig, which was no better than a bathing machine, plunged into it, and all the forward part of her was under water, the sea pouring in through the bow ports and hawse holes and over the knightheads, threatening to wash everything overboard. In the lee scuppers it was up to a man's waist. We sprang aloft and double-reefed the topsails and furled the other sails and made all snug. But this would not do; the brig was laboring and straining against the head sea, and the gale was growing worse and worse. At the same time sleet and hail were driving with all fury against us. We clewed down and hauled out the reef tackles again and close-reefed the fore-topsail and furled the main and hove her to on the starboard tack. . . .

182

Throughout the night it stormed violently—rain, hail, snow, and sleet beating upon the vessel—the wind continuing ahead and the sea running high. At daybreak (about three a.m.) the deck was covered with snow. The captain sent up the steward with a glass of grog to each of the watch. And all the time that we were off the Cape grog was given to the morning watch and to all hands whenever we reefed topsails. . . .

Sunday, November 9th. . . . A true specimen of Cape Horn was coming upon us. A great cloud of a dark slate color was driving on us from the southwest, and we did our best to take in sail (for the light sails had been set during the first part of the day) before we were in the midst of it. We had got the light sails furled, the courses hauled up, and the topsail reef tackles hauled out and were just mounting the fore-rigging when the storm struck us. In an instant the sea, which had been comparatively quiet, was running higher and higher, and it became almost as dark as night. . . .

At this instant the chief mate, who was standing on the top of the windlass, at the foot of the spencer [try-sail] mast, called out, "Lay out there and furl the jib!" This was no agreeable or safe duty, yet it must be done. John, a Swede (the best sailor on board) who belonged on the forecastle, sprang out upon the bowsprit. Another one must go. It was a clear case of holding back. I was near the mate, but sprang past several, threw the downhaul over the windlass, and jumped between the knightheads out upon the bowsprit. The crew stood abaft the windlass and hauled the jib down while John and I got out upon the weather side of the jib boom, our feet on the foot ropes, holding on by the spar, the great jib flying off to leeward and *slatting* so as almost to throw us off the

183

boom. For some time we could do nothing but hold on, and the vessel, diving into two huge seas one after the other, plunged us twice into the water up to our chins. We hardly knew whether we were on or off when, the boom lifting us up dripping from the water, we were raised high into the air and then plunged below again.

John thought the boom would go every moment and called out to the mate to keep the vessel off and haul down the staysail. But the fury of the wind and the breaking of the seas against the bows defied every attempt to make ourselves heard, and we were obliged to do the best we could in our situation. . . .

Thursday. The same. We had now got hardened to Cape weather, the vessel was under reduced sail, and everything secured on deck and below, so that we had little to do but to steer and to stand our watch. Our clothes were all wet through, and the only change was from wet to more wet. There is no fire in the forecastle, and we cannot dry clothes at the galley. It was in vain to think of reading or working below, for we were too tired, the hatchways were closed down, and everything was wet and uncomfortable, black and dirty, heaving and pitching. We had only to come below when the watch was out, wring our wet clothes, hang them up to chafe against the bulkheads, and turn in and sleep as soundly as we could until our watch was called again.

A sailor can sleep anywhere—no sound of wind, water, canvas, rope, wood, or iron can keep him awake—and we were always fast asleep when three blows on the hatchway and the unwelcome cry of "All Starbowlines ahoy! Eight bells there below! Do you hear the news?" (the usual formula of calling the watch) roused us up from our berths upon the cold, wet decks.

The only time when we could be said to take any pleasure was at night and morning, when we were allowed a tin pot full of hot tea (or, as the sailors significantly call it, "water bewitched") sweetened with molasses. This, bad as it was, was still warm and comforting, and, together with our sea biscuit and cold salt beef, made a meal. Yet even this meal was attended with some uncertainty. We had to go ourselves to the galley and take our kid of beef and tin pots of tea and run the risk of losing them before we could get below. Many a kid of beef have I seen rolling in the scuppers, and the bearer lying at his length on the decks.

Dartmouth, one of the nine colonial colleges, was established originally as a school for Indians. By the 1830's it had the impressive appearance illustrated in this Currier lithograph after A. B. Young [n.d.]. *Courtesy, Library of Congress.*

Chapter 10

Getting an Education

Education for the rank and file of Americans has been a problem vexing the nation from its beginning. Most thinking members of the population agreed with James Madison that "a people who mean to be their own governors must arm themselves with the power which knowledge gives," but there the agreement ended. It was easy to say that education was a good and necessary thing for every youth; it was quite another matter to pay for such an educational system, and nobody in the early days had the influence to impose a national scheme of education, though many political leaders talked about it. Schooling in the decades after independence limped along much as it had during the colonial period. New England towns, for example, generally had adequate (but not necessarily free) schools; while rural areas often made do with what were called old field schools.

Thomas Jefferson set forth an elaborate plan for an educational system from kindergarten through the university which envisioned a selection at various levels of the most promising students for further education at the expense of the state. His plan would have created an aristoc-

Typical of the "little red schoolhouse" that played such an important part in the education and social life of the nineteenth century is this first public school of Alton, Illinois, shown as it appeared in 1866. The girls have remained discreetly inside. *Pen-and-ink drawing by A. N. Houghton, 1897, from an earlier view. Courtesy, Library of Congress.*

racy of intelligence, which he believed necessary for the success of a democratic society. But neither Jefferson's nor any later generation has been willing to adopt this principle of selection on the basis of talent. In recent times anyone suggesting the creation of an intellectual elite would be charged with fascism or some other unholy doctrine. So schools muddled along, as they have muddled ever since, not being quite certain of what they wanted to do or how to do it.

Many patriots in the early days of the Republic were convinced that Americans ought to free themselves of foreign influences, particularly dependence upon Britain for schoolbooks and educational ideas. During the colonial period many boys had gone to England or Scotland for education. Now Americans argued that the country must provide colleges that would make transatlantic study unnecessary, a view that resulted in the establishment of scores of academies and colleges in the next half century.

One of the most ardent advocates of American education for Americans was Noah Webster, a Connecticut Yankee and graduate of Yale, who set out to Americanize the spelling, pronunciation, and diction of his fellow countrymen. If he tried to make them pronounce their words with a Connecticut twang, that, he believed, was much better than letting them sound like Englishmen. To work his miracle, he published spelling books, readers, and eventually a dictionary which became the nation's standard work of lexicography. His *Compendious Dictionary of the English Language,* first published in 1806, was followed in 1828 by a two-volume work, *An American Dictionary of the English Language.* Although others published dictionaries, Webster's quickly gained and held the ascendancy. To Webster's determination to be un-British we owe the simplification of such words as "plow" instead of "plough," "labor" instead of "labour."

For a couple of generations, however, Virginians and some other Southerners preferred John Walker's *A Critical Pronouncing Dictionary and Expositor of the English Language,* first published in 1791, for it seemed to them more elegant than Webster's with its insistence on a Connecticut pronunciation. Walker conceded the correctness, for instance, of the Virginian pronunciation of "gyarden" for garden.

Webster's famous spelling books, commonly called *Blue Back Spellers,* had their beginning immediately after the close of the Revolutionary War with the publication of a combination reading book, speller, and grammar entitled *A Grammatical Institute of the English Language* (1783–85). The first portion of this work was published separately as his spelling book, which continued in circulation for most of the nineteenth century. Throughout the country spelling matches, sometimes called spelling bees, gained a popularity that they retained for a century. Sometimes adults, sometimes schoolchildren, would choose sides and stand opposite each other. A master of ceremonies would give out the words, first to one side and then to the other. Whenever anyone misspelled a word, he had to sit down. The side with the most survivors after a given period of time was the winner. And always Webster's *Blue Back Speller* was the authority. Such was the popularity of this textbook that by 1890 some 60,000,000 copies had been sold.

Noah Webster, of course, was not the only patriotic textbook maker. The Reverend Jedidiah Morse, for example, another citizen of Connecticut, believed that we ought to have a geography that centered interest in North America. To provide such a work, he published in 1784 *Geography Made Easy*, followed by other geographical texts from which for many years schoolboys learned about the great world. Morse, like Webster, gave his books a slant distinctly influenced by his Connecticut outlook; for example, he claimed that "North America has no remarkably high mountains. The most considerable are those known under the general name of the Allegany Mountains."

Local patriotism often resulted in adapting textbooks to a particular region or state. For example, printers in frontier Kentucky brought out Samuel Wilson's *The Kentucky Grammar* (1797), *The Kentucky Primer* (1798), and *The Kentucky Spelling-Book* (1798). A book that Abraham Lincoln is said to have studied was *The Kentucky Preceptor Containing a Number of Useful Lessons for Reading and Speaking* (1812). The publication of textbooks was a lucrative business, then as now, and printers throughout the country sought to reach local markets with books that appealed to special interests.

The most famous of all textbooks of the nineteenth century were the *Eclectic Readers* compiled by William Holmes McGuffey, which he began to publish in 1836 while president of Cincinnati College. It is estimated that some 122,000,000 copies of these reading books have been sold, and the favorite, *McGuffey's Sixth Eclectic Reader*, is still in print in a paperback version. From 1836 to 1860 McGuffey's *Readers* provided food for thought, selections for speeches, and poetry and prose chosen to please, as well as to instruct. Many a youngster received his first—and sometimes only—taste for good literature from the selections in McGuffey's *Readers*. Few books have had such a profound influence upon a generation. Published in Cincinnati, they were the most widely used textbooks in the Midwest and found acceptance in other parts of the country as well.

McGuffey, like most educators of his time, believed that schools should develop character and that textbooks should be moralistic. Hence his *Readers* provided material that conveyed good lessons of some sort, albeit the selections were all interesting as well. Some of the most famous passages from great writers were included. For example, the *Sixth Reader* had a number of excerpts from Shakespeare. Schoolboys could find—and memorize—Henry V's speech to his soldiers before the Battle of Agincourt or some other appropriate passage to their liking. But lest they miss the moral lesson in another passage, a scene from *Othello* (Act II, Scene ii) giving the dialogue between Iago and the drunken Cassio, McGuffey headed it "The Folly of Intoxication."

Public recitations were a part of every schoolchild's education, and a book that provided proper speeches was prized. McGuffey's *Sixth Reader* was ideal in this respect. A boy could choose something stirring, say Patrick Henry's "Speech Before the Virginia Convention"; a girl could find a bit of verse, perhaps Samuel Woodworth's poetic tribute to skill in sewing called "The Needle," the last stanza of which reads as follows:

> Be wise, then, ye maidens, nor seek admiration
>   By dressing for conquest and flirting with all;
> You never, whate'er be your fortune or station,
>   Appear half so lovely at rout or at ball,
> As gayly convened at the work-covered table,
>   Each cheerfully active, playing her part,
> Beguiling the task with a song or a fable,

And plying the needle with exquisite art:
The bright little needle, the swift-flying needle,
The needle directed by beauty and art.

The book contained a great variety of material, all appropriate for any occasion, all informative and improving. Friday afternoon was the usual time for the delivery of recitations, and every schoolhouse rang with oratory, frequently learned from McGuffey's *Sixth Reader*. Such lessons in public speaking helped train future politicians and statesmen.

Going to school before the Civil War, whether in erudite Boston or backwoods Tennessee, was a different procedure from that which students know today. No buses gathered up children and conveyed them to schools equipped with every convenience. Pupils frequently walked distances of several miles in all weathers, carrying their books and lunch buckets in their hands. Few schools were free; no truant officers checked up to see that children were in class instead of on the streets, for education was not compulsory, though here and there efforts were made to induce parents to see that their children at least learned to read, write, and "cipher." Schools were not yet divided into grades. Unlike the present day, the teacher was frequently a man, sometimes fresh out of college, teaching for a year or two before going on to study law or medicine.

In the country most schoolhouses had only one or two rooms. While the teacher heard the lesson of the younger pupils, the older ones were supposed to study. To see that they did and to enforce discipline generally, the teacher kept a quantity of birch rods standing in the corner with which he thrashed unruly youths when they deserved it. Public opinion was not yet sympathetic to misbehavior, and parents often announced that a child who got a whipping at school could expect another when he got home.

Pupils in the advanced classes were almost as old as and sometimes bigger than the teacher. A famous American teacher told of accepting a post at a school where a bully boasted that he had "run off" every previous teacher. On the first day of school the bully deliberately provoked the new teacher, a muscular type, who promptly whipped the hulking youth and expelled him. The next day the boy's parents came begging to have him let back in school. After much pleading the mother made a final appeal: "Willy ain't really a bad boy," she declared. "Leastways, he ain't never cussed his Pa at the table."

Only gradually did the notion of free elementary and secondary education for everybody catch on. Even in New England, where schools were the most advanced in the country, public opinion held that parents able to pay should not expect education for their children at the expense of the taxpayers, though it was agreed that towns should provide free schools for the poor. In 1834, however, Pennsylvania passed a law establishing a free school system for rich and poor. No longer would poor children be made to feel that they were objects of charity. But the law created a storm of protest from taxpayers unwilling to supply free schooling for well-to-do children. Nevertheless, despite efforts to repeal the law, it stood and in time was imitated by other states. By the middle of the century many states had well-organized educational systems; some had a superintendent of education who made efforts to raise the standards of both schools and their teachers.

As yet there were practically no requirements for teacher training. Any young man or woman with the rudiments of a college education—sometimes with only one or two years of college—could get a job teaching. The pay was meager, often supplied by fees paid by parents, but in pre-inflation times a little money went far. In many instances teachers received less than a dollar a day. In the country part of the teacher's pay was in the form of board in the homes of people who had children in school; after a few weeks in one home he (or she) moved on to the next. There was no lack of opportunity for "communication" between teacher, parents, and children.

In the South during the colonial period many school-masters had come from Scotland, for the Scots were noted for their learning and conscientiousness. In the first half of the nineteenth century the Scots were replaced by young men from New England colleges. Eli Whitney, for example, the inventor of the cotton gin, went from Yale to Georgia to be a tutor in the family of General Nathanael Greene. Some of these New Englanders married and remained in the South.

Despite the slowness with which the states adopted systems of free schools, by the mid-century elementary schools of all types required the services of some 90,000 teachers to instruct well over 3,300,000 pupils. The secondary schools of the country had more than 12,000 teachers and more than 250,000 pupils. Not all these schools were supported by taxation, but the number of free schools had grown remarkably, and few pupils need grow up without an opportunity of learning reading, writing, and arithmetic, the fundamentals of elementary education. A scattering of public high schools in the larger towns, and many private academies, some supported by religious groups, offered more advanced courses that frequently included Greek and Latin; a classical background was believed essential for a well-educated man. Young women might attend one of the numerous female academies, where they were taught the refinements that a woman of the day was expected to know: music, a little art, and a smattering of what we would call the humanities, chiefly literature.

With the learning picked up in one of the secondary schools, a determined youth need not lack a college education, for numerous institutions were available, and entrance was easy. No college boards, no entrance examinations, and no high school diplomas were required. Usually a recommendation from a former teacher and an interview with the president or some other official of the college were sufficient to admit a student to the freshman class. The older colleges—Harvard, Yale, Princeton, William and Mary,

Oldest institution of higher education in the nation, Harvard in colonial times boasted three "colledges" housed in Harvard Hall, Stoughton Hall, and Massachusetts Hall, shown here as they appeared about 1725. The college attained university status in 1780. *Engraving by William Burgis, 1740. Courtesy, Library of Congress.*

and others—were hardly more formal than the newest institutions in the West.

In the first half of the century some eighty new colleges were founded throughout the country, an incredible record, even though many of these institutions could boast only two or three professors housed in a single building. Many owed their beginning to religious denominations which believed that colleges could help Christianize the community. As in the colonial period, colleges were also needed to ensure a supply of preachers. Yale and Princeton sent out many educational leaders who founded little colleges all the way across the continent. For example, in 1828 a group of devout young Yale graduates banded together and vowed to devote themselves to the salvation and education of Illinois. In the next year the "Yale Band" founded Illinois College at Jacksonville. In similar fashion preachers and

195

teachers established other colleges throughout the West. Oberlin, founded in 1833, was one of the most distinguished of these early colleges; it was the first to open its doors to two minority groups, blacks and women. Coeducation was a new departure in American higher education.

If a young man wanted to be a lawyer or a doctor, he had two choices: He could attend one of the few professional schools, or he could apprentice himself to an established member of the profession. Most lawyers and doctors in the period before the Civil War followed the latter procedure.

Some lawyers provided for their clerks and apprentices what amounted to a course in law and turned out numerous

One of the earliest of the women's colleges was the Georgia Female College at Macon, as classical in its Greek Revival architecture as in its course of studies. *Engraving in William C. Richards, Georgia Illustrated, 1842, after a drawing by Hinshelwood. Courtesy, Library of Congress.*

members of the bar, some of whom rose to high place. In Virginia, George Wythe numbered Thomas Jefferson among other noted Virginians who received their legal training under him. In New England, Tapping Reeve at Litchfield, Connecticut, and successors in his firm conducted what amounted to a law school. An archconservative, Reeve inoculated his students with strong Federalist doctrines. This Litchfield law office eventually could count among its alumni fifteen United States Senators, ten governors, two Supreme Court Justices, and forty judges of other jurisdictions. John C. Calhoun of South Carolina acquired his legal training at Litchfield.

But a lad with legal ambitions did not have to sit at the feet of a George Wythe or a Tapping Reeve, for every country lawyer took in youngsters who could read enough of Blackstone's *Commentaries* to pass the cursory examinations of local bar associations and hang out their shingles. Of course, formal training in law was not unknown in the colleges and universities; the best-known law schools were those at Harvard, the University of Virginia, and Transylvania University at Lexington, Kentucky.

Medical education was hardly more formal than legal training. The better-known medical schools were found at Harvard, the College of Philadelphia (the University of Pennsylvania), Transylvania University (for a time), and the short-lived Ohio Medical College at Cincinnati. Courses in medicine, however, were soon offered at many colleges which have long since abandoned them. Sometimes the entire medical faculty consisted of one man who gave lectures. For more than a decade, for example, Professor Nathan Smith was Dartmouth's sole instructor in its medical school.

Dissection and anatomical study were almost as primitive as they had been in the Renaissance, when Vesalius reformed medical education at the University of Padua. For many years the only bodies legally available for dissection were those of condemned criminals; in 1830 Massachusetts finally passed a law permitting the unclaimed bodies of paupers dying in public institutions to be used. Unable to find cadavers, some medical schools depended on grave robbers, a nefarious business that aroused public indignation and sometimes caused riots. Body stealing involving a Yale professor required a military guard to save him from the mob.

Like an incipient lawyer, an ambitious boy could apprentice himself to a physician and learn enough to pass the examination for a license to practice. Many physicians kept their favorite prescriptions secret and only transmitted them to their apprentices, who graduated into junior partners. In the frontier regions more than one quack, without benefit of education or license, set up shop and prescribed for the sick.

Americans, then as now, worried about their health and dosed themselves with countless nostrums called patent medicines because their secret formulas had been patented. The first American to patent a pill was a Connecticut Yankee named Samuel Lee, Jr., who obtained in 1796 government protection for his famous Bilious Pills, which claimed to be useful against "yellow fever, jaundice, dysentery, dropsy, worms, and female complaints." Lee, like a long list of medicine vendors down to the present day, discovered the value of advertising to such effect that soon people were demanding his Bilious Pills, and imitators were infringing his patent. During the next half century hundreds of patent medicines would advertise their extravagant claims to cure the ailments of men and women and would make fortunes for their manufacturers. Interestingly, in view of modern concern about the intake of mercury, Samuel Lee advertised that his pills contained no mercury, for mercury preparations were popular in this day. One of the favorite prescriptions of doctors for more than a century was calomel (mercurous chloride), which anyone who ever had to take it would be glad to avoid.

Before the Civil War a young man who wanted to be an

engineer was best advised to go to the United States Military Academy at West Point, oldest of the service academies. The small American Army could not absorb all the officers graduated from West Point, and many entered business or set up as private engineers. The modern demand of students for "relevant" studies is not new. Students in every age have probably felt that much that they studied had little relation to their current interests. In the last decade of the eighteenth century a controversy raged over the relevance of the emphasis on classical learning. Some opponents of Latin and Greek argued that the study of these ancient pagan languages would induce immorality and weaken Christian faith. Defenders of the classics quickly pointed out that Americans could not afford to be ignorant

Patent medicines were among the first products to profit substantially from advertising that was more exotic than accurate. Nostrums of reputed Indian or Oriental origin enjoyed particular success; among them was "Old Sachem Bitters Wigwam Tonic," advertised as inducing the vigor of an Indian chief. *Lithograph by Sarony, Major & Knapp, 1859. Courtesy, Library of Congress.*

First of the service academies, the U.S. Military Academy at West Point opened its doors to cadets on July 4, 1802. This is a view from upriver in the 1830's. *Aquatint by W. J. Bennett, 1834, after a painting by George Cooke. Courtesy, Library of Congress.*

of the civilizations that had contributed most to their heritage. But the controversy has continued to crop up from time to time down to the present day.

College students of the first half of the nineteenth century were not unlike modern students in other respects. They found fault with their living quarters, their food, their teachers, and their studies. They also caused frequent riots. Colleges did not dream of intercollegiate athletics or physical education programs to absorb energies of students with too much time on their hands, although students themselves organized ball games of various kinds, which sometimes ended in free-for-all fights.

A Jesuit priest, Giovanni Grassi, who came to this country in 1810 and published a book on his travels in 1819, reported on the riotous nature of college students as follows:

When they [young Americans] reach a certain age they become impatient with suggestions, at least with those that do not coincide with their own. The liberty that they assume often descends to insubordination and to violent revolts against superiors. Such uprisings are not unusual in American colleges, and have lately occurred in Princeton in New Jersey and in William and Mary in Virginia; the students broke windows, chairs, furniture, and everything that came to their hands, and were at the point of destroying the very buildings. Since the people who preside over such places are concerned only with the injection of a little knowledge into the students, it is not surprising that the latter bring themselves to certain excesses of misbehavior which are condemned by honest Americans.[1]

Whatever the shortcomings of American schools and colleges in the years before the Civil War, most Americans somehow managed to acquire enough learning to fit them for whatever places they occupied in society. Many an American, Abraham Lincoln being perhaps the best-known example, contrived by his own efforts to educate himself. Lincoln's successor in the Presidency, Andrew Johnson, is said to have been illiterate to the time of his marriage; indeed, he may have married his wife in order to have her teach him to read and write. However that may be, he set himself to learn and educated himself so well that he rose from a North Carolina tailor shop to the highest office in the United States.

A keen desire for learning drove countless Americans to educate themselves. The very difficulties of getting an education may have made it more precious to nineteenth-century Americans. They wanted to rise above the common ruck of mankind, and their best hope was through some form of schooling, whether formal or self-contrived. Not many were affluent, and nobody yet insisted that everybody needed, or should have, what came to be known as a literary education. Those whose interests and talents led them into trades and crafts served apprenticeships and learned the required skills. Education of a higher sort was for those who wanted it and could obtain it by their own hard work.

Chapter 11

Going to Church

Religion played an enormous role in the lives of most nineteenth-century Americans, a role that the present generation has difficulty appreciating. Even the unreligious were profoundly affected, for an effort to resist religious pressures sometimes brought them into violent conflict with the pious. The village atheist might find himself ostracized and his business ruined. Even so, nearly every community had an apostate or two; blacksmiths, for reasons hard to understand, were often among the unorthodox minority who occasionally delighted in irritating neighbors and customers. The religiosity of the majority of Americans in the first half of the nineteenth century did not ensure peace, for denominational controversies raged. Even within denominations, particularly among the Presbyterians, doctrinal arguments resulted in disputes, acrimony, and division. The very arguments over religion, however, tended to confirm Americans in whatever their beliefs might be and to induce them to build churches, hire preachers, and eventually to send out missionaries to convert the heathen.

The Puritanism of the colonial period did not die a

natural death, for it had a vitality that has kept it going, albeit with constant modifications, until the present time. At the end of the Revolution Congregationalists of New England were among the most staunchly conservative of Americans, and they looked upon all things French, particularly after the excesses of the French Revolution, as evil influences threatening the very foundations of American society. Timothy Dwight, president of Yale, called "Pope Dwight," railed against the French who would place a strumpet goddess of reason on the altars of Jehovah and substitute a "Jacobin frenzy" for "our holy worship."

Many Americans in high place had abandoned the strict piety of their ancestors for a mild sort of rationalism that can be described as deism, a rationalism that fanatical Puritans equated with the doctrines of the French Revolution. Consequently Dwight and other Congregationalists preached against the iniquity of following foreign beliefs destined to bring disaster upon the nation. They might have been less excited, for the mass of Americans continued to go to churches of their faiths and were not conspiring to overthrow the Republic. But the concern of conservative Congregationalists in New England illustrates the way that religion affected the lives and political fortunes of Americans.

The publication in 1796 of Tom Paine's *Age of Reason* popularized deistic ideas of earlier English writers and philosophers which conceded a supreme being but denied divine revelation and the supernaturalism accepted by orthodox Christians. As one might have expected, the pious described Paine as a limb of Satan; and as one also might have anticipated, college students immediately adopted Paine as the prophet of a new dispensation. To read and quote Paine's *Age of Reason* marked a young man as an "intellectual." Although for a decade or two deistic beliefs gained adherents, the vogue of deism gradually faded before the onslaughts of orthodox writers and preachers who warred against these "infidels." Nevertheless, few communities lacked one or two unbelievers who delighted in annoying the overly righteous with arguments endlessly propounded, in winter, around the stove of the general store and in summer under the trees shading benches on the town square or village green. Religion, or the lack of it, provided the theme for perennial discussion and debate.

One of the rights guaranteed by the First Amendment to the Constitution was freedom of religious belief. No longer need citizens fear a national established church supported by taxation, and no longer could the law require a citizen to go to church. Although previously a few colonies had tried to maintain an established church, in reality a diversity of religions managed to flourish. After independence nothing except local community pressure prevented anyone from preaching whatever doctrine pleased him.

In the years after the Revolution churches which had been controlled from England—for example, the Episcopal, the Methodist, and the Roman Catholic (supervised by a vicar apostolic in London)—gradually established their American autonomy with leaders of their own choosing. The consecration of bishops in proper apostolic succession at first proved a vexing problem for Episcopalians, but in time the Church of England relented and consecrated men who had been rebels against the king.

In New England the Congregationalists, natural heirs of seventeenth-century Puritanism, had long been the prevailing denomination, but in the first half of the nineteenth century many joined the Episcopal Church, which was more relaxed and fashionable. To the older Congregationalists this defection was alarming, but what was far worse was the desertion of some of the faithful to the heresies of Unitarianism and Universalism.

Someone has defined a Unitarian as "one who believes, at the most, in one God." It was also said that the Unitarians held that God was too good to damn any man and that the Universalists believed that man was too good for God to damn. Before the end of the eighteenth century

205

Unitarians and Universalists were gaining adherents, both in the towns and in the backcountry, to the new heresy that man no longer need fear hell because of Adam's sin and his own innate depravity—a cardinal doctrine of Puritanism. A more comfortable religion naturally had an appeal for men and women who had been terrified from childhood by the awful threat of hellfire awaiting them.

Harvard became a stronghold of Unitarianism, to the scandal of the orthodox who congratulated themselves that Yale, under "Pope Dwight," still knew right from wrong. To combat heresy and "infidelism," Congregationalists and Presbyterians became more militant and evangelical. The Episcopalians, on the other hand, took little part in fervid campaigns against heretics; secure in their belief in the benignity of God, they appealed to many well-placed members of the community.

From colonial times Pennsylvania had welcomed men of all religious beliefs and had within its borders citizens of many religions. William Penn, himself a member of the Society of Friends (Quakers), had made his colony a haven for his fellow religionists, who continued to flourish after the beginning of the national period. Quaker businessmen in Philadelphia were noted for their acumen, their sound business principles, and their integrity. Other religions, sharing Quaker beliefs in a spiritual inner light and a hatred of war, also came to Pennsylvania in large numbers. These included German-speaking Mennonites, Dunkers, and other sectarians from the Rhineland. Peaceful Moravians settled around Bethlehem and were noted for their educational work and missionary efforts. Many German Lutherans also came to Pennsylvania and later sent settlers westward.

In all the states Baptists and Methodists, imbued with evangelical zeal, made many converts and increased enormously in the first half of the century. They appealed particularly to less sophisticated folk in the small towns and the backcountry, for their doctrines were plain and understand-

The sobriety and industriousness of Quakers, or Friends, which contributed so much to the early prosperity of Pennsylvania, is apparent in this contemporary portrayal of a group on their way to meeting, or church. Note the absence of sleigh bells. *Engraving in Robert Sutcliff,* Travels in Some Parts of North America, 1811. *Courtesy, Library of Congress.*

able; they were not encumbered with ritual; and their preachers were for the most part plain people themselves, sometimes with hardly more education than their backwoods converts.

The Baptists had an advantage over other denominations because they had no central organization to dictate policy. Any group of converts could organize a church, call a preacher, and manage their affairs as they saw fit. In rural districts the preachers themselves were often local farmers who had heard a call to expound the gospel and save souls. Donning a black suit on Sunday, the preacher mounted the pulpit, called out the hymns, and gave an exhortation based on some favorite scriptural text. In the summer when the crops were laid by, these farmer-preachers might ride to more distant churches and join in a series of revivals designed to renew the spiritual convictions of rural America. Since the revival was often the most exciting event of the summer, it drew most of the populace, both saints and sinners. In the country and even in the towns, men and women of other denominations joined in the revival services. Both Baptists and Methodists emphasized revivals as a potent means of reaching the unregenerate, as well as renewing the fervor of those already saved.

The Methodists were noted for their circuit riders, preachers who, with a few tracts in their saddlebags,

207

"In weather like this only crows and Methodist preachers would be out." A circuit rider making his rounds. Wood engraving in Harper's Weekly, October 12, 1867, after a drawing by A. R. Waud. Courtesy, Library of Congress.

mounted their horses and rode great distances to reach congregations that otherwise would have lacked spiritual nour-
ishment. When the weather was bitter in the winter, Westerners would sometimes say, "In weather like this only
crows and Methodist preachers would be out." Nothing
stopped the circuit riders, not weather, not poverty, not
threats of bullies and badmen. They went where they believed sinners needed saving, they scattered tracts, they
prayed with the sick and buried the dead, and they sometimes heard the lessons of children learning to read. The
impact of these fearless preachers in the backcountry would
be hard to overestimate. Like the Baptists, the Methodists
conducted revivals that sometimes reached a high emotional pitch. The term "shouting Methodist" originated in
emotional outbursts of members of the congregation.

Unlike the Baptists, the Methodists had a highly struc-
tured organization with a bishop at the top and with presid-
ing elders to supervise districts within the jurisdiction.
Preachers were moved every four years to a different pas-
torate and were thus known as an itinerating ministry. This
constant shift gave Methodist preachers a wide knowledge
of people and places. Few villages, towns, or country districts lacked the attention of a Methodist preacher who
could bring to his mission a comparative knowledge of
other regions. Many of these preachers developed great skill
as pulpit orators. If they encountered a hostile audience,
they could hold their own with quick repartee—or with
sheer muscle if force should be required. Methodist preachers, particularly on the frontier, were not to be taken
lightly. A favorite popular hymn of the Methodists exempli-
fied their militant attitude toward sin and ungodly free
thinkers:

> The world, the devil, and Tom Paine
> Have done their best, but all in vain;
> They can't prevail, the reason is:
> The Lord defends the Methodists. . . .

They pray, they preach, they sing the best,
And do the devil most molest;
If Satan had his vicious way,
He'd kill and damn them all today.

Presbyterians also played an important, but a somewhat different, role in the first half of the nineteenth century. They were organized into presbyteries subordinated to larger synods, and they insisted on an educated ministry. It was said that the Presbyterians believed that a minister would have to give the password into heaven in Latin or Greek. Certainly the Presbyterians were responsible for large numbers of classical academies and colleges.

The most distinguished Presbyterian dignitary of the early period was Dr. John Witherspoon, a Scottish minister who became president of Princeton before the Revolution, was a signer of the Declaration of Independence, and exerted so much influence on his fellow religionists that for a time he helped reconcile warring factions within the church. Witherspoon also made Princeton a seedbed of classical learning for the rest of the country. Presbyterian preachers swarmed out from Princeton, taking their Greek and Latin grammars with them and establishing schools that insisted on the value of classical training. They are credited with founding forty-nine colleges by 1860, not to mention numerous academies. Although the Presbyterians led in the number of colleges founded, other denominations were also active in providing for higher education, which they believed to be a means of man's moral improvement and ultimate salvation. According to the leading historian of religion in America, W. W. Sweet, in the same period the Methodists opened 34 colleges, "the Baptists 25, the Congregationalists 21, the Catholics 14, the Episcopalians 11, the Lutherans 6, the Disciples 5, the German Reformed and the Universalists four each, the Quakers and Unitarians two each, the Dutch Reformed and the United Brethren one each."[1]

Perhaps because the Presbyterians put greater emphasis upon theological doctrine than some of the other evangelical denominations, they were susceptible to disputes about the finer points of dogma. Their controversies rocked the church during the first third of the century, and once again, as in the colonial period, Presbyterians were arrayed against Presbyterians as "Old School" conservatives fought "New School" liberals. One of the points in dispute was the question of revivalism which the "New School" advocated and practiced. More fundamental was the concern over the acceptance of the Westminster Confession of Faith and the belief in Calvinistic predestination. During the 1830's the conservatives brought many preachers before church boards and charged them with heresy. Feeling ran so high that whole groups separated into new denominations. The Disciples of Christ, sometimes called Campbellites, and the Cumberland Presbyterians were offshoots from the older Presbyterian Church. The Associated Reformed Presbyterians, sometimes called Seceders, broke off in 1822. Spiritual descendants of an extremely conservative element in the Scottish church, they forbade instrumental music in religious services and confined their singing to psalms. Other sectarian divisions also occurred in the church.

Religious controversy was so common in the first third of the nineteenth century that a quarrel even split the Quakers into two sects. Beginning in 1823, the Yearly Meetings of the Quakers in Philadelphia saw a growing contention between wealthy city members and those from the country over evangelical doctrines which the more conservative country Quakers did not approve. Leader of the conservatives was Elias Hicks. In 1827 the followers of Hicks withdrew from the Philadelphia Meeting and formed a group soon known as Hicksites to distinguish them from the older, more liberal, orthodox party. The Hicksites were numerous in the Middle West.

The religious ferment in the first half of the century resulted in the rise of numerous new sects. For some reason upper New York State proved a fertile ground for religious speculation. Among sectarian groups originating there, two were particularly notable: the Mormons and the Seventh Day Adventists.

In 1831 Joseph Smith announced that he had found in the Hill of Palmyra golden plates containing the text of the Book of Mormon. Quickly gaining followers, he moved headquarters to Kirtland, Ohio; Smith and most of his disciples went on to Independence, Missouri, and other nearby localities. When they came in conflict with Missouri "gentiles," they picked up again and settled in Nauvoo, Illinois, which by 1842 they had built into the largest city in the state. Their political power and beliefs strange to their neighbors soon aroused such hostility that Smith and his brother Hyrum were arrested. On June 27, 1844, a mob stormed the jail at Carthage, Illinois, and lynched both of them. The Church of Jesus Christ of Latter-Day Saints, as the Mormons called themselves, now faced a dilemma. With their prophet gone and a hostile mob threatening them, they elected Brigham Young their leader and decided to leave the beautiful city they had built and find another haven in the West. Not all the faithful agreed to follow Young. A minority elected a brother of Joseph Smith their head and called themselves the Reorganized Church of Jesus Christ of Latter-Day Saints. They too left Nauvoo but settled elsewhere in the Middle West.

Young turned out to be a great leader of men—and of women. In the summer of 1847 he led the first Mormon pioneers across the plains to Utah and selected the valley of Great Salt Lake as the site of their future Zion. During the next three years the Mormons laid out Salt Lake City and began the conquest of the desert; in an incredibly short time they had a prosperous and well-governed territory. Until his death in 1877 Young remained the head of the church and the strongest political leader in Utah.

The doctrine of plural marriages, promulgated in 1852 on the basis of a vision vouchsafed Joseph Smith in 1843,

212

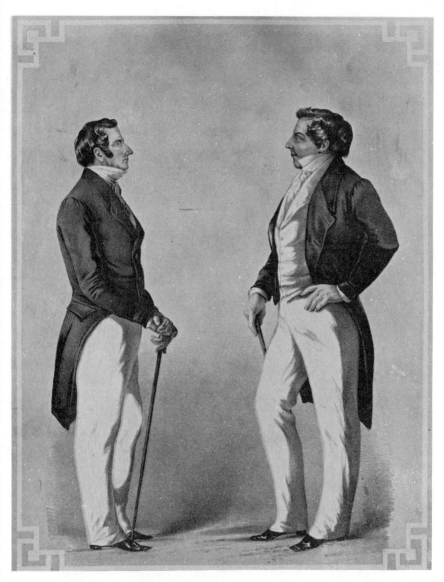

Two unlikely looking martyrs: Joseph Smith, founder of the Church of Jesus Christ of Latter-Day Saints, and his brother Hyrum. Their assassination in 1846, resulting from growing prejudice against the Mormons, helped induce the mass migration to Utah. *Lithograph by Sarony & Major, 1847. Courtesy, Library of Congress.*

created a storm outside Utah. Newspapers and free-lance writers soon blanketed the country with sensational articles on Mormon polygamy. Eventually the federal government had to intervene to forbid the practice. Actually, polygamy was an economic and social solution of the problem of an excess of women in the Mormon society. Eager missionaries had made many converts in America and abroad, especially among women, and hundreds had come to Utah from England and elsewhere. In a frontier society they needed the protection of husbands and homes. Polygamy was the answer. Brigham Young himself married at least twenty-six women, each of whom had a house in Young's compound in Salt Lake City. Over them he presided with the dignity and authority of a Biblical patriarch.

The Mormon doctrine of plural marriages gave rise not only to criticism, but to an insatiable public curiosity about the settlement at Salt Lake City. Newspapers and magazines were quick to profit from both. This engraving of Brigham Young and his wives and children on their way to church appeared in *Harper's Weekly* for October 10, 1857. *Courtesy, Library of Congress.*

The Seventh-Day Adventists had their origin in the beliefs set forth by William Miller, who grew up in Hampton, New York. A pious Baptist, he read the Scriptures diligently and thought he found convincing evidence that the world would end in 1843. In 1839 Miller converted to his beliefs a Baptist preacher named Joshua Vaughan Himes, and the two set out to warn the world of the imminence of the Second Coming of Christ.

Himes proved to be one of the most effective publicists of his day. In 1840 he founded in Boston a newspaper, *Signs of the Times*, which broadcast the message as did *The Midnight Cry*, another paper that he began publishing in New York two years later. By 1843 thousands of believers were fearfully waiting for the great day, which did not come as predicted. Miller revised his calculations, and the papers announced that the day would be October 22, 1844.

Again the faithful prepared for the end of the world as they had known it. Men left their work, farmers abandoned their crops, and women performed only routine duties to keep households going. On the eve of October 22 crowds in many parts of the country gathered again to await the event. Some, dressed in white robes, met in the open and shivered through the autumn night. Although October 22 passed uneventfully, the believers remained unshaken in their faith. Miller and Himes agreed that their calculations for a specific date had been wrong but that Christ was coming soon at an indefinite time.

At a meeting in Albany in 1845 their followers organized a church which has become known as the Seventh-Day Adventists. They celebrate as the Sabbath the day beginning at sunset on Friday and ending at sunset on Saturday. The Seventh-Day Adventists in the modern world have emphasized service to mankind, particularly medical service, and their medical missionaries have made notable contributions in many backward areas.

The Mormons and the Seventh-Day Adventists were only two of a number of new faiths that evolved in the period.

Camp meetings retained their popularity through the nineteenth century and into the twentieth. The above scene was
a camp session held at Sing Sing (later Ossining), New
York, in August, 1859. Note emotional expressions and at-
titudes of the two women in center foreground. *Wood engraving in* Harper's, *September 10, 1859. Courtesy, Library
of Congress.*

They illustrate the vitality of religious beliefs and the ease
with which new doctrines developed among people who
read their Bibles and felt competent to make their own in-
terpretations.

Religion provided excitement and entertainment, as well
as spiritual comfort. In every community the churches, of
whatever persuasion, were centers that ministered to the social needs of their congregations. For women, particularly,
church work gave an outlet for activities that relieved the

tedium of household duties. Church suppers brought together people of various social levels and made a bright spot for many who otherwise would have had little opportunity to mix informally in such affairs. Sunday school picnics appealed to the young and provided an opportunity for decorous courting. It would be hard to overestimate the importance of the country church in the social development of nineteenth-century Americans.

The most exciting times came during revivals when emotions reached a high pitch, both in city and country churches. Young people crowded to services which had a theatrical appeal as noted reprobates heeded the warnings of damnation and rose to tell of their repentance. There was much hymn singing and congregational participation as lay exhorters moved about the church, pleading with hardened sinners to "give their hearts to God." At a certain point in the service the preacher would usually ask all who wanted to be saved to stand up or to come forward to the mourners' bench just beneath the pulpit. Old and young, emotionally stirred, would thus express their desire for salvation. One could be sure that the town drunk would be "converted," for every revival reached one or two such recalcitrants. Within a few weeks he would backslide, but for the time being he could bask in the approval of the godly.

Early in the century a movement that came to be known as the Second Awakening swept the country. This was a series of spiritual revivals somewhat like the Great Awakening of the mid-eighteenth century. Shortly after the Revolution, at two small Presbyterian colleges in Virginia (later called Hampden-Sidney and Washington and Lee), students underwent a religious experience that led a number to enter the ministry and go out to the frontier as missionaries. This was the earliest manifestation of a religious fervor that soon swept through other colleges, Presbyterian and Congregational, and eventually spread widely throughout the populace. During the first two decades of the new century revivalism stirred the whole country.

This era saw the development of the camp meeting as a means of reaching vast throngs of country people. Perhaps the first genuine camp meeting was held in Logan County, Kentucky, in 1800, and in August, 1801, according to W. W. Sweet, "the greatest of all recorded camp meetings was held at Cane Ridge, Bourbon County, Kentucky, and was planned by another of the converts of the Hampden-Sidney revival."[2]

At a typical camp meeting people came from far and near, pitched tents under the trees, and settled down for a week or more of preaching. As many as a half dozen or more preachers took turns exhorting the multitude from a pulpit erected under a brush arbor. Prayers began early in the morning, followed by breakfast and the morning sermon. After a noontime dinner came another sermon in the afternoon. A respite and supper were followed by a third sermon delivered in the evening.

Since the preachers were often skillful orators capable of painting vivid pictures of the torments in hell awaiting the unsaved, they induced hysterics in some of their hearers. Men and women would occasionally fall frothing at the mouth or give way to moans and cries for help. Volunteers from the congregation would undertake to comfort the distressed and to assure them that God would forgive the truly repentant.

Unsympathetic observers and sensational writers made much of the emotional excesses of the camp meetings which sometimes provided opportunities for sexual indulgences not conducive to salvation as the exhorters represented it. That such excesses sometimes occurred is unquestioned, but Sweet insists that the better preachers tried to curb emotionalism and frowned upon their brethren who drove congregations to hysterics.

One of the most famous of the camp meeting preachers was a Methodist, Peter Cartwright, who did his best to maintain order and decorum at his meetings. Sometimes in backwoods areas rowdies would try to break up services. At such a meeting in 1806 at Marietta, Ohio, a group of young ruffians appeared with knives and horsewhips and began a disturbance. Cartwright stopped his sermon and asked for order. When even justices of the peace who were present seemed afraid to intervene, Cartwright marched from his pulpit, approached the leader of the mob, and knocked him out cold. With that the congregation helped him round up thirty toughs, who were fined heavily before being released. That ended disorder at the Marietta camp meeting.

How much camp meetings did to bring salvation to rural America may be a moot question, but no one can deny that they brought excitement to the participants and were a diversion that thousands appreciated. The evidence is clear that many people underwent genuine conversions that lasted. The camp meeting was an effort to meet the spiritual needs of people who may have failed to respond to, or have been unable to participate in, formal church services.

Another manifestation of the religiosity of the first half of the century expressed itself in the missionary movement, both domestic and foreign. Preachers described the plight of Indians going to hell without benefit of salvation, and soon societies were organized to preach the Gospel to the red man. The first American settlers in Oregon were led by a Methodist missionary, Jason Lee, who settled in the Willamette Valley in 1834. He was soon followed by others, including Dr. Marcus Whitman, a medical missionary, and two Presbyterian preachers, Samuel Parker and H. H. Spaulding, who settled in the Walla Walla Valley. Despite a frontier belief that the only good Indian was a dead one, home missionary societies back East sent out a number of preachers to carry the word to the aborigines.

Foreign missions also created much interest in this period. The trade with China naturally focused attention upon the Far East. Contacts with Africa attracted others to that region. A few even thought of trying to spread the gospel of Protestantism to Catholic South America. At any rate, in 1810 under the influence of students from Andover

Theological Seminary the American Board of Commissioners for Foreign Missions was organized. Its influences would be far-reaching, and its messages about the need of the heathen for salvation would stir American imaginations for generations.

The most colorful of the early missionary undertakings was the effort to take salvation to Hawaii. Hawaii (or the Sandwich Islands, as this region was then called) was already well known to whalers and China traders. In 1809 a whaling captain brought to New Haven two native Hawaiian boys whom he called Henry Obookiah and Thomas Hoopoo. With two heathen in their midst, Yale theological students went to work to fill them with learning and religion. Soon other Hawaiian youths arrived in New Haven and were induced to attend a mission school opened at Cornwall, Connecticut. Their sponsors hoped that they would go home and convert their countrymen.

Stories of the wickedness of the Hawaiians told by the boys and by whalers themselves so worked up would-be missionaries in Connecticut that in 1819 they organized a missionary band to go out and save them from perdition. The leaders were Hiram Bingham of Middlebury College and Asa Thurston of Yale. On September 29, 1819, at a service at Goshen, Connecticut, they were ordained and dedicated to the Hawaiian mission. The sermon on this occasion was entitled "The Promised Land," and the text was from Joshua (13:1): ". . . and there remaineth yet very much land to be possessed." Presently others were recruited for the expedition, which sailed on October 23, 1819. The story of the Christian conquest of Hawaii has no place in the present chapter, but the stories sent back did much to stir other laborers in the mission vineyard.[3]

Reports of returned foreign missionaries were exciting to young people, who eagerly listened to the tales they told of exotic peoples and distant places of the earth. Many a home-keeping youth got his first and only insight into foreign life from these missionary talks at the local church.

The religious spirit of the period also resulted in a great outburst of reform movements and the organization of societies to improve morals, induce temperance, distribute Bibles, free the slaves, and perform countless other virtuous deeds. The desire to "do good" was rampant in many communities and became a part of American nature. This tendency has not yet disappeared, and many Americans continue to think of themselves as their brothers' keepers.

The original campus of the University of Virginia, designed by
Thomas Jefferson, with its open colonnades lining a large quad-
rangle and templelike structure at the far end, had the appearance
of a Roman forum—an excellent example of classic influence on the
young republic. *Engraving by Benjamin Tanner, 1826. Courtesy,
Library of Congress.*

Chapter 12

Enjoying Life

From the arrival of the first colonists until the present time, most Americans have dreamed of an improved status that would permit a greater enjoyment of life. Precisely what this improved status meant has varied from time to time and place to place, but usually it has included the hope of a better home, a larger income, and more leisure for recreation of one sort or another. During the 1960's a few young people, generally middle-class and affluent, reversed this age-old ambition and decided that their dream of a better life meant abandoning the trappings of conventional civilization, going barefoot, wearing nondescript clothes, and "returning to nature." This tendency is not entirely new, for it has cropped up at intervals among unrealistic romantics, but it has never been a prevailing trend. Over the years the first essential that most Americans have demanded has been a comfortable home.

During the first half of the nineteenth century the desire for better homes was evidenced by an outburst of house building throughout the country. A long tradition had already established conservative styles of solidly built, utili-

Solidity and good design characterized the home, outside and in, of the early Pennsylvania Germans, famous for their folk art. The fireplace wall of this room from a Berks County farmhouse built in 1783 is decorated with *Fractur*, a medieval German art of illuminated writing. More familiar, perhaps, are the floral and unicorn designs framed on the far walls and painted on dower chests under the windows. *Photograph. Courtesy, The Henry Francis du Pont Winterthur Museum.*

tarian dwellings, some of considerable attractiveness, in all the colonies. New England's compact saltbox style houses were adapted to the cold climate; New York's step-gabled dwellings continued a style introduced by the Dutch; Philadelphia had handsome four-square structures, as well as gracefully designed brick buildings that we would describe as Georgian. The Pennsylvania Germans had solidly built gray stone houses flanked by immense barns. The plantation houses of the South, some of brick but most of wood, followed no conventional pattern. Thus, before the turn of the century, the nation demonstrated not only its variety but a desire for excellence in domestic architecture. That desire would increase with every increment of prosperity gained by its citizens.

Thomas Jefferson, himself an architect of no mean ability, illustrated in his home, Monticello, the interest of the late-eighteenth and early-nineteenth centuries in classic form—the use of Greek and Roman themes—which characterized many of the finer dwellings, as well as famous public buildings of the period. He declared that architecture was of prime importance and urged Americans to maintain good taste in so conspicuous an art. To practice what he preached, Jefferson designed houses for his friends. He was also responsible for the plan of the State Capitol in Richmond and the original structures of the University of Virginia in Charlottesville, two of the best examples in America of the adaptation of classic form to public buildings.

But it would be a mistake to believe that America suddenly blossomed with classic mansions for the wealthy and Greek Revival public buildings. Numerous as these were, they did not tell the whole story. Southern plantation houses were not even typically the white-columned structures of fiction and the motion pictures. The majority of dwelling houses were far simpler in construction, for few professional architects were available to the nation at large; most dwelling houses—and even public buildings such as courthouses and schools—were the handiwork of local carpenters. Sometimes they had pattern books; more often they worked from a simple sketch made by the landowner or depended on their own imaginations.

In the South the ordinary plantation house was normally a two-storied affair with a chimney at each end, a hall down the middle, an "el" for extra bedrooms and kitchen, and a porch stretching across the front. More often than not the roof of the porch was held up by cedar posts instead of imposing columns. A few fine Greek Revival dwellings existed, it is true, especially in the sugar-rich districts of Louisiana and elsewhere in the South, but they were the exception and not the rule.

All over the country, however, men were seeking to improve their dwellings and to fill them with the comforts, the

In political discussion and in architecture the Founding Fathers consciously recalled Republican Rome. Americans were less conscious, perhaps, of Roman precedent in their early preoccupation with plumbing. The above advertisement for luxurious bathroom appointments, including hot and cold running water and a shower, was published in 1844 for a plumbing firm that boasted of being "established in New York A.D. 1835." *Lithograph by Endicott after J. Galwey. Courtesy, Library of Congress.*

amenities, and the decorations that fashion decreed. Wealthy merchants in Boston, Salem, New York, Newport, Providence, Philadelphia, Charleston, or any other trading port built new houses or added to those they had inherited. They bought excellent furniture, some imported from England or France, some made by a growing number of native craftsmen. The Henry Francis du Pont Winterthur Museum at Wilmington, Delaware, provides abundant visual proof of the skill of American craftsmen and artists and the taste displayed by Americans on various social levels before the mid-century.

Trade with China had an extraordinary impact upon taste in the early national period, as Americans sought originality in household furnishings. Chinese porcelains, Chinese wallpaper, Chinese art objects, Chinese furniture suddenly became popular. The English furniture designer Thomas Chippendale had come under Chinese influence, and Americans bought many pieces of Chinese Chippendale furniture.

Not merely were the simplicity of classic form and the elegance of Oriental art admired in early America; a romantic interest in the Middle Ages resulted in the appear-

226

The Gothic turrets of the first Smithsonian building, rising on the Washington Mall in 1852, introduced medieval romanticism in strange contrast with the stately classic orders of the capital city. A contemporary description noted that it was "the first edifice in the style of the twelfth century and of a character not ecclesiastical ever erected in this country." *Lithograph by Sarony & Major (n.d.). Courtesy, Library of Congress.*

ance of turreted buildings suggestive of ancient castles. The old Smithsonian Building in Washington, D.C., is probably the best-known survival of this Gothic style. But the crenellated structure was not confined to public buildings. Dwelling houses with round towers, useless turrets, and all manner of gingerbread decorations around the eaves were common. Unhappily any ingenious carpenter could create the Gothic excrescences that characterized many dwelling houses. The elaborate work of the scroll saw with which many simple houses fairly dripped at the beginning of the present century marked the final deterioration of the crenellated Gothic style.

Not every American could afford a fancy dwelling, but all wanted the most comfortable house he could achieve. Much depended upon his geographical location. Dwellers in log cabins on the frontier boarded over their chinked logs as soon as sawmills made planking available. Prairie settlers in Nebraska, ready at first to exist in houses of turf and sod, rebuilt their homes with lumber as soon as a railroad came within hauling distance. Farmers once content with unpainted wooden shacks rebuilt and painted them, often under the persuasion of wives conscious of appearances.

European travelers who commented, often unfavorably, upon the unceasing labor of Americans and their unrelieved pursuit of money failed to realize that money was only a means to an end, and that end was a better life. Each generation hoped to improve on the past. Every parent hoped to give his children better opportunities than he had had. That, at least, was the general attitude; as in all societies, a few varied from the norm, and most communities had shiftless ne'er-do-wells who lacked ambition for self-improvement. In some backwoods areas, notably in the Appalachians, squatters lived in primitive innocence of "book larnin'," which they scorned.

Although long hours of hard work were the lot of most Americans, they subscribed to the old adage that all work and no play makes Jack a dull boy. Nowhere, not even among plantation slaves, was amusement completely lacking. In some fashion everyone contrived to find alleviation from the humdrum routines of the daily struggle to survive or to get ahead. Yet even the amusements frequently had some productive utility. For example, women gathered for quilting parties where finishing an article needed by the family gave an opportunity for the exchange of gossip.

Entertainment varied with the locality and with the sophistication of the inhabitants of a particular region. The older cities of the East could boast theaters, concert halls, bookstores, libraries, and a few museums. Even small towns in the West soon opened theaters, and traveling companies of actors brought popular drama to the hinterland. San Francisco, for example, became the focal point for theatrical companies during the gold rush.

Although a few religious groups frowned on theatrical entertainment as "worldly" and therefore wicked, playgoing was popular throughout the country. When professional companies were not available, amateur groups organized and performed for their own and their neighbors' amusement. In every region Shakespeare was a favorite. Boston,

One of the earliest theaters in the nation, Boston's Haymarket Theater was literally located in a hay market. *Reproduction of an undated watercolor by Archibald Robertson. Courtesy, Library of Congress.*

New York, Philadelphia, Charleston, and New Orleans already had long traditions as theatrical centers. The early opposition of the Puritans in Boston and the Quakers in Philadelphia had not prevented the rise and prosperity of the theaters in those cities. Unlike the present time, with its movie theaters and television, nearly every town of any consequence, even in raw frontier areas, erected theaters and attracted touring companies of actors. More legitimate drama was seen by Americans before 1860 than has been seen in the present century.

The hardships of travel did not deter distinguished actors and actresses from visiting out-of-the-way places in America. British companies made frequent trips across the Atlantic and then across the expanse of this continent. American companies competed with the foreigners, and traveling

229

A women's equivalent to a "house raising" (pictured above), for which neighboring men came in to help build, was the quilting party, or bee—an opportunity to socialize while getting assistance with the making of quilts for bedding. Blankets were expensive, and quilts could be made at home from scraps. Moreover, they were decorative and provided one of the few opportunities for artistic expression. Note the rifle and powder horn hanging ready over the door. *Engraving in* Gleason's, *October 21, 1854. Courtesy, Library of Congress.*

companies reached towns so small that today they would not have a motion-picture theater. During the first twenty years of the nineteenth century theatrical companies frequently appeared at the river towns of Kentucky; Louisville especially was noted for plays. Shakespeare remained the most popular dramatist, and the favorite plays were *Richard III, Othello, Hamlet, The Taming of the Shrew, The Merchant of Venice, Romeo and Juliet, Much Ado About Nothing,* and *King Lear* in that order. But one should not jump to the conclusion that Shakespeare was the only dramatic fare appealing to Americans. They also liked blood-and-thunder melodrama and plays dripping with sentimentality. For instance, such a crude performance as William Henry Smith's *The Drunkard*, first produced in

Boston in 1844 and advertised as "A Moral Domestic Drama," had a long run. A dramatic version of Harriet Beecher Stowe's abolitionist novel *Uncle Tom's Cabin*, adapted by George L. Aiken and first performed on September 27, 1852, in Troy, New York, ran for 100 nights and remained popular in the North for many years.

Audiences, however, were offered many other diversions besides conventional drama. Traveling exhibitions of every conceivable sort appealed to their interest, from medicine shows selling rattlesnake oil guaranteed to cure rheumatism to a "professor" demonstrating an electric machine. The most famous showman of the age was P. T. Barnum, who combined talent and fakery and contrived to make a fortune out of American gullibility. To him is attributed the cynical comment "There's a sucker born every minute."

The "New Theatre" opposite Congress Hall in Chestnut Street was popular with early Philadelphians, to judge by this contemporary engraving in William Birch & Son, *The City of Philadelphia*, 1800. This view was taken from in front of the State House (Independence Hall), looking along Chestnut Street in the opposite direction from the view on page 110 (Chapter VII), with the same public pump in the foreground. *Courtesy, Library of Congress.*

Barnum's American Museum (building on left, with flag), which
the showman acquired in 1841, had a prime location on Broadway at Ann Street, facing two long-standing New York land-
marks: St. Paul's (center), oldest church in the city, and Astor
House (right), hotel of the rich and the famous. In St. Paul's
churchyard was buried the first English actor of star rank to come
to America, George Frederick Cooke of the Theatre Royal, Drury
Lane, who made his first U.S. appearance at nearby Park Theater
in 1810 and died in 1812. Cooke's gravestone was kept in repair
by a succession of notable actors, including Edwin Booth in 1890.
Guests at Astor House included Andrew Jackson, Henry Clay,
Daniel Webster, Jenny Lind, and Abraham Lincoln. *Lithograph
published by Hoff & Bloede, 1850. Courtesy, Library of Congress.*

Barnum gained his first notoriety in 1835 by exhibiting
an aged black woman, said to be a hundred and sixty-one
years old, as "George Washington's nurse." Making as
plausible a story as possible, he coached his exhibit to cooperate by telling of the youth of little George. Once
launched on his career as an exhibitor of curiosities, Barnum improved his repertory with a "bearded lady," a "Fee-
jee mermaid," and countless other attractions, animate and
inanimate, to interest a naïve public. One object, for example, was a war club brought back by a whaler from Hawaii which Barnum described as the very weapon that
killed Captain James Cook.

Traffic jams are not a new experience in New York. This impasse of sleighs at Broadway and Ann Street illustrates the excitement generated by the well-advertised attractions at Barnum's Museum in the 1850's. *Lithograph by Nagel & Lewis, 1855, after D. Benecke. Courtesy, Library of Congress.*

In 1841 Barnum bought a hodgepodge collection in New York called the American Museum and proceeded to add to its curiosities. Museums of this period were usually nondescript assortments of this and that—weapons and utensils used by the Indians or some savage tribe of the South Seas, Chinese objects brought back by traders, bones of mastodons or other extinct animals, some genuine historic articles, some sheer fakes, anything, in short, that the exhibitor thought might conceivably be of interest. In his autobiography Barnum noted that he "labored to keep the Museum well supplied with transient novelties; I exhibited such living curiosities as a rhinoceros, giraffes, grizzly bears, orangoutangs, great serpents, and whatever else of the kind money would buy or enterprise secure."[1] He had earlier had some experience with a small traveling circus, and much later he was to become one of the partners of an attraction advertised as "The Greatest Show on Earth," Barnum and Bailey's Circus.

Barnum did not confine his entertaining efforts to curiosities and circuses. In 1850 he was the impresario who brought over the famous Swedish singer Jenny Lind. He arranged for her a triumphal tour through the nation, including New York, Boston, Philadelphia, Baltimore, Richmond, New Orleans, Louisville, Cincinnati, Pittsburgh, and other cities and towns. With advance advertising of "the Swedish Nightingale" Barnum created enormous excitement; the singer was often nearly mobbed by crowds press-

233

Barnum's "Swedish Nightingale," Jenny Lind, as she appeared in the title role of Donizetti's *Le Fille du Régiment* in 1850. The opera, written in Italian under the title of *La Figlia del reggimento* (1840), was revived at New York's Metropolitan Opera House in 1972 after a lapse of many years. *Lithograph by Sarony, 1850. Courtesy, Library of Congress.*

ing to see her as she arrived at her hotel. Concerts were sold out in advance, and people clamored for tickets. The reception of Jenny Lind was proof both of the American love of music and of the power of advertising.

That the public enjoyed music had already been proved by the popularity of touring companies of musicians. In 1848 another Scandinavian, the Norwegian violinist Ole Bull, made a tremendous hit on an American tour. In the same year a German orchestra introduced Wagner's music, and the Revolution of 1848 in Germany resulted in many other German musicians coming to this country. In 1847 the Havana Opera Company, said to have been the finest opera company up to that time to perform in the United States, received such a welcome that it returned the following year. By the middle of the century few towns having a theater or concert hall lacked musical entertainment.

Formal groups, however, were not the only evidence of American musical interest. Everywhere singing was popular, and itinerant singing masters were common even in frontier communities. On the arrival of a singing teacher in a community everyone capable of carrying a tune gathereᴅ

Stephen Foster, composer of nostalgic songs of the old South, including "Old Folks at Home" ("Swanee River") and "Old Black Joe," was born in Lawrenceville, Pennsylvania, and went south of the Mason and Dixon Line only once. He made a study, however, of black music, which gave his own compositions their folk song quality. *Photograph of a painting by Clough [n.d.]. Courtesy, Library of Congress.*

at the schoolhouse or church for lessons and practice. Using a popular songbook, perhaps Lowell Mason's *The Boston Glee Book* (first published in 1838), they learned simple melodies that were sentimental, patriotic, and sometimes humorous. Nor were hymns and other religious songs neglected by the singing classes, for they were sometimes even more popular than secular music.

One of the favorite songwriters of the mid-century was Stephen Foster, a Cincinnati bookkeeper, whose work is still remembered. He composed a number of songs for black minstrel shows, which were another form of popular theatrical entertainment in this period. Before the end of 1854 his publishers had sold more than 130,000 copies of "Old Folks at Home" and 90,000 copies of "My Old Kentucky Home." Another favorite from his pen was "Old Black Joe." Emigrants headed for California in search of gold

The popularity of lectures as entertainment seasoned with edification can be seen in the size and appointments of the lecture room of Barnum's American Museum. The entertainment illustrated, however, suggests that the hall was also used for dramatic presentations. *Wood engraving by Avery after Chapin in* Gleason's, *January 29, 1853. Courtesy, Library of Congress.*

sang "Oh! Susanna," and "Jeanie with the Light Brown Hair" may still be heard. Americans did not lack for tuneful airs, which they sang on every occasion.

The public's favorite musical instrument of that day was the fiddle, not the guitar, though sometimes the banjo ran the fiddle a close second. Country fiddlers played for square dances, and at the sound of "Turkey in the Straw" feet began to twitch. Because of the use of the fiddle at dances and other folk festivals certain of the pious referred to it as "the devil's instrument." The objection of the overly righteous, however, did not diminish the popularity of the fiddle and the dances that it set in motion.

Americans have always found satisfaction in the pleasures believed to be improving, a tendency that accounts for the popularity of lectures. Beginning in the 1820's, a movement for mutual improvement developed into what became known as the lyceum system—series of subscription lectures first started in New England. The trend rapidly spread until by the mid-century a town without a lyceum stood in danger of being called backward, if not barbarous. The lectures were informative or inspirational and served as a potent means of adult education, as well as for popular

236

entertainment. The most famous of all the lyceum lecturers was Ralph Waldo Emerson, but many other prominent writers, scientists, and political figures traveled the lyceum circuit and entertained audiences throughout the land. The oratory of Daniel Webster rang from the lyceum platform, as well as in the United States Senate chamber; this was an age that reveled in the spoken word, the more eloquent and resounding the better, and Webster was a past master as a spellbinder. People would travel for miles to hear a famous orator. Even college oratorical contests attracted eager crowds. The lyceum platforms helped satisfy this public appetite for eloquence.

Busy as were Americans in the first half of the nineteenth century, they found time for satisfaction in reading. Boston was the literary center of the nation, well equipped with bookstores and with publishers. But other cities also laid

Fashion, then as now, was a topic of universal interest and a staple of news and special publications. London and Paris, arbiters of high style for gentlemen and their ladies, produced these creations for summer wear in 1845. *Aquatint published by T. Oliver, 1845. Courtesy, Library of Congress.*

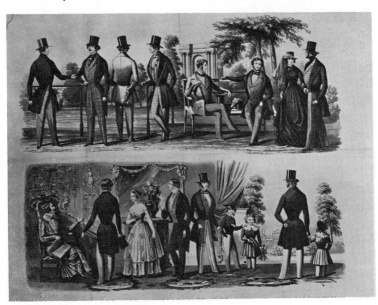

Ralph Waldo Emerson, most famous and influential of all the lyceum lecturers, as he appeared in the 1850's. *Lithograph by John H. Bufford after L. Grozelier, 1859. Courtesy, Library of Congress.*

claims to a high degree of literacy. From colonial times Philadelphia had had numerous printers, publishers, and booksellers. New York was already the base for a growing number of publishers. And in the West, Cincinnati was a focal point for both publishing and book distribution.

In thousands of homes families were accustomed to gather around the lamp in the living room while someone read aloud, perhaps from one of Sir Walter Scott's novels, from Dickens, or maybe a bit of Byron's poetry, though Byron in the opinion of some was hardly a fit writer for the fireside. Be that as it may, Byron was exceedingly popular. Both Scott's prose and poetry were so well known and liked that steamboats were named after his heroes and heroines. Family reading of the Bible was common, and the rhythms of the King James Version influenced many a writer and speaker. Abraham Lincoln read the Bible by the light of blazing pine knots to the great improvement of his own style. Before the days of radio and television family gatherings to read aloud some entertaining or improving work helped maintain domestic solidarity.

Magazines and newspapers contributed to the entertainment of the populace. For the sophisticated, *Harper's*

Monthly Magazine, founded in New York in 1850, was the most important source of literary essays, especially selections from current British authors. For women and the family as a whole, *Godey's Lady's Book*, which began publication in Philadelphia in 1830, served as the criterion of taste and fashion. Not only did it publish illustrations of the latest styles and other material of interest to women, but it included stories and essays by leading American writers of the time. *Godey's Lady's Book* was widely read and enjoyed by both men and women and had an important impact upon American culture. If *Godey's Lady's Book* presented the acme of Eastern elegance, the West was not to be outdone. Cincinnati had its *Ladies' Repository*, established by the Methodists in 1841, a magazine designed to keep women instructed in religion and to provide literary pieces deemed proper for feminine eyes. Chicago's *Lady's Western Magazine* made an effort to be both elegant and proper. Other magazines also discovered the feminine market and stressed articles and fiction appealing to women. No television dispensed soap opera in this age, but periodicals dished up sentimental tales that were the equivalent.

Not all publications aimed at audiences concerned with elegance or moral improvement. In 1845 *The National Police Gazette*, known later as "the barbershop Bible," began a long career of supplying sensational news of crime, divorce, and scandal generally. Before nudity became commonplace, the *Police Gazette* featured on its pink pages thinly clad girls, particularly those caught in some violation of the law. Newspapers making claims to greater respectability than the *Police Gazette* were hardly less sensational. In 1833 Benjamin H. Day founded the New York *Sun*, a penny daily that emphasized entertaining local news and startling stories to hold the interest of the multitude. Its most famous scoop was a complete hoax, published in August, 1835, purporting to be a summary of discoveries on the moon by the British scientist Sir John Herschel. Basing its "facts" on a fictitious article in a Scottish scientific journal that had already ceased publication, the *Sun* described moon men and animals in graphic detail. So convincing were the stories that a group of scientists from Yale were sufficiently impressed to ask to see the sources, and for a time the public accepted the startling revelations of life on the moon as veritable truth. When the paper revealed the hoax, the public laughed at the joke—and at scientists who, they believed, had proved equally gullible. The hoax inspired Edgar Allan Poe to attempt in "Hans Pfaall" a story of a moon voyage. The *Sun's* moon hoax had a modern parallel in Orson Welles' radio broadcast of an alleged arrival on earth of beings from Mars.

Benjamin Day's *Sun* soon had competition from another sensational penny paper, the New York *Herald*, established in 1835 by a Scot, James Gordon Bennett, who tried to outdo the *Sun* in stories intended to amuse, entertain, and gain subscribers. Bennett was a proslavery advocate until the Civil War, when he switched to vigorous espousal of the Union.

Other newspapers in New York and elsewhere throughout the country catered to the growing public appetite for news. Nearly every country town had its paper, some edited by talented men who wrote vigorously and well, others got out by printers barely literate—or sober—enough to set type and clip from other papers the news they published. Many of these country papers depended for much of their revenue on advertisements of patent medicines promising to cure all ailments afflicting men and women, for in this age no government agency policed advertising of drugs or anything else. Many men and women found their principal enjoyment of the local paper in reading symptoms of diseases and the printed testimonials of their cures.

The first half of the nineteenth century was not without sports, but they had not yet become commercially organized, and they played a much smaller role in life than at present. For one reason, the public had less leisure. Colleges made little effort to stimulate physical education,

Skating and sledding were popular and inexpensive sports where winter weather permitted. *Currier lithograph, 1856, after F. F. Palmer. Courtesy, Library of Congress.*

though a few had gymnasiums and encouraged a limited number of interclass games. Football was not unknown, but it was an altogether different game from the one we know and often ended in a free-for-all fight. Bowling enjoyed much greater popularity than football, but it was for the most part still a masculine sport. In urban regions favored with quiet rivers, rowing became a social attraction. Hunting and fishing, of course, were almost universally enjoyed, but in cities the favorite outdoor activity of many young dandies was buggy riding behind high-stepping horses. They could then invite girls to accompany them.

The 1850's, however, saw the rise of baseball to national importance. Previously boys had played ball in cow pas-

An early manifestation of Women's Lib was the bloomer costume illustrated here, a daring innovation of early 1851 popularized by Amelia Bloomer, editor of a feminist journal. The fad for bloomers among the avant-garde disappeared with the revival of the hoopskirt! *Currier lithograph, 1851. Courtesy, Library of Congress.*

tures and old fields, but by 1858 baseball had become of such general interest that the National Association of Baseball Players was organized to make rules that would apply generally. Soon towns had teams to compete with each other, and baseball was on its way to becoming the favorite sport of Americans.

In the North ice skating in winter was one of the few outdoor sports in which both men and women could take part. In 1857 Thomas Wentworth Higginson, in the newly founded *Atlantic Monthly*, wrote an article entitled "Saints and Their Bodies" advocating physical exercise for both men and women; he particularly stressed skating and continued to commend it until critics began to sneer at his preachments as "Higginson's revival." Skating gave women an opportunity to wear "bloomers" (baggy pants), then a daring innovation.

On a few beaches, particularly at Newport, swimming in mixed company attracted growing interest. But women had to be careful to shroud themselves in bathing suits that reached from neck to ankles and included a flowing skirt that effectively concealed the female form. Even so, men contrived to enjoy teaching their girl friends to swim, a tutelage that gave an opportunity at least to balance the lady delicately while she paddled and splashed. A few beaches strictly segregated the sexes. Sometimes a beach would hang out a red flag to warn that men were bathing nude and no modest maiden should approach.

Spectator sports played a less conspicuous part in life then than now. Horse racing, to be sure, had long supplied excitement in the South and certain parts of the North, notably in Rhode Island, which was an old horse-breeding region. But even horse racing appealed to only a relatively small portion of the population. On a lower level, cockfighting in some parts of the South and West drew small crowds

"Swimming" in mixed company was also for the daring—in bloomerlike bathing costumes that swathed the female form from neck to ankle. Coney Island was already in the news as the appropriate setting for "sea bathing illustrated." *Wood engraving in* Frank Leslie's Illustrated Newspaper, September 20, 1856. *Courtesy, Library of Congress.*

Horse racing was becoming popular in some sections of the country as a spectator sport involving large sums of money. In this illustration Peytona noses out Fashion "for $20,000!!!" —an enormous purse for the time—on the New York Union racetrack on May 13, 1845. *Lithograph by J. Baillie, 1845. Courtesy, Library of Congress.*

eager to bet on the winner. Boxing and wrestling matches were common at county fairs, militia drills, and similar gatherings. Occasionally these boxing matches developed into barefisted prizefights when combatants beat each other into bloody pulps before whooping crowds that cheered them on.

Prizefighting was not regarded, however, as a respectable sport, and often matches were staged surreptitiously. Moralists complained that prizefights represented a degenerate form of brutality imported from England. Despite the disapproval of the better element, occasional prizefights drew crowds, but neither the numbers in attendance nor the money involved approached the magnitude of modern

244

times. One fight, however, staged outside New York in 1860, drew 30,000 spectators, a phenomenal outpouring for such an event.

The search for amusement, entertainment, and improvement became more intense as Americans increased in wealth and as more people found time for recreation, diversion, and useful avocations. One pleasure that now became more attractive was travel. Both Europe and America drew numbers of tourists eager to see the wonders of their own or foreign lands. Railroads eased the burdens and hardships of journeys that once had repelled all but the most hardy. Steamships made foreign travel quicker, cheaper, and less hazardous. As a result, Americans poured from their hives and, like bees in search of nectar, swarmed over Europe and their own country.

No longer was wealth essential for some sort of journey merely for pleasure. The railroads saw to that. Advertising cheap "excursions" to nearby hot springs, scenic spots, or to a city offering urban attractions, special trains carried thousands who rode just for the fun of it, some merely for the excitement of traveling on "the cars."

A few resorts drew the most fashionable. Saratoga Springs, New York, Newport, Rhode Island, and Hot Springs, Virginia, catered to the wealthy and the socially established. Newport was a focal point for rich planters from the South who were accustomed to summer there. Indeed, it became a veritable Southern colony, and its cotillions were famous for the beauties who danced there.

But as the controversies that wracked North and South toward the end of the period grew more bitter, Northerners proved less hospitable and Southerners more sensitive to criticism and slights. By 1860 they were deserting Newport and seeking recreation in their own region. Although political arguments grew more bitter, in the summer of 1860, as ladies and gentlemen sat rocking and fanning themselves on hotel porches, few would have predicted that the search for enjoyment of life within another year would give way to the horror of civil war. None then knew that 1860 was the end of an era.

Notes

Chapter II

1. Charles D. Hazen, *Contemporary American Opinion of the French Revolution* (Baltimore, 1897), p. 164. Subsequent quotations concerning similar celebrations are from the same work.
2. *Ibid.*, p. 183.
3. Margaret Bayard Smith, *The First Forty Years of Washington Society*, Gaillard Hunt, ed. (New York, 1906), pp. 310 ff.
4. *Ibid.*, pp. 294 ff.
5. Samuel E. Morison and Henry S. Commager, *The Growth of the American Republic* (New York, 1942), vol. I, p. 556.

Chapter III

1. John C. Miller, *The Federalist Era* (New York, 1960), p. 156.
2. *Ibid.*, p. 150.
3. Morison and Commager, *op. cit.*, vol. I, p. 376.
4. Smith, *op. cit.*, p. 101.

Chapter IV

1. Augustus John Foster, *Jeffersonian America: Notes on the United States of America*, Richard B. Davis, ed. (San Marino, Calif., 1954), p. 20.
2. *Ibid.*, p. 84.
3. *Ibid.*, p. 87.
4. *Ibid.*, p. 138.
5. *Ibid.*, p. 130.
6. Frances Trollope, *Domestic Manners of the Americans*, Donald Smalley, ed. (New York, 1949), p. 45.
7. *Ibid.*, p. 16.

8. *Ibid.*, p. 58.
9. *Ibid.*, p. 234.
10. *Ibid.*, pp. 18–19.
11. *Ibid.*, p. 85.
12. *Ibid.*, p. 121.

Chapter V

1. Foster, *op. cit.*, p. 139.
2. Quoted in Warren S. Tryon, ed., *A Mirror for Americans* (Chicago, 1952), vol. III, pp. 572–73.
3. *Ibid.*, vol. III, pp. 512–13.
4. Trollope, *op. cit.*, p. 17.
5. *A Mirror for Americans*, vol. I, p. 110.
6. Michael Chevalier, *Society, Manners, and Politics in the United States*, John W. Ward, ed. (New York, 1961), p. 74.
7. *Ibid.*, p. 76.

Chapter VI

1. Trollope, *op. cit.*, p. 43.
2. *Ibid.*, p. 301.
3. *Ibid.*, pp. 120–21.
4. Freeman Hunt, *Worth and Wealth* (Chicago, 1883), p. 38.
5. *Ibid.*, pp. 653–55.
6. *Ibid.*, pp. 603–04.
7. Alexis de Tocqueville, *Democracy in America*, trans. by George Lawrence (New York, 1966), p. 47.
8. *Ibid.*, p. 597.
9. Quoted by Irvin G. Wyllie, *The Self-Made Man in America* (New Brunswick, N.J., 1954), p. 14.
10. *Ibid.*, pp. 14–15.
11. *Ibid.*, p. 15.
12. *Ibid.*, p. 27.

Chapter VII

1. *Moreau de St.-Méry's American Journey, 1793–1798.* Edited by Kenneth Roberts and Anna M. Roberts (New York, 1947), p. 331.
2. *Ibid.*, pp. 324–25.

3. *Ibid.*, p. 255.
4. Robert G. Albion, *The Rise of New York Port* (New York, 1970), p. 253.
5. *Ibid.*, p. 241.
6. Chevalier, *op. cit.*, p. 138.

Chapter VIII

1. Quoted by Morison and Commager, *op. cit.*, vol. I, p. 246.
2. Quoted by J. H. Easterby, *The South Carolina Rice Plantation as Revealed in the Papers of Robert F. W. Allston* (Chicago, 1945), p. 57.
3. Kenneth Stamp, *The Peculiar Institution* (New York, 1956), p. 30.

Chapter IX

1. James H. Young, *The Toadstool Millionaires* (Princeton, 1961), pp. 173–75, 200.
2. Quoted by Edouard A. Stackpole, *The Sea-Hunters* (Philadelphia, 1953), p. 318.
3. A. B. C. Whipple, *Yankee Whalers in the South Seas* (New York, 1954), p. 66.

Chapter X

1. Quoted by Oscar Handlin, *This Was America* (Cambridge, Mass., 1949), p. 143.

Chapter XI

1. W. W. Sweet, *Religion in the Development of American Culture* (New York, 1952), p. 165.
2. *Ibid.*, p. 149.
3. See Louis B. Wright and Mary Isabel Fry, *Puritans in the South Seas* (New York, 1936), pp. 269–321.

Chapter XII

1. Quoted from Phineas T. Barnum, *Barnum's Own Story*, Waldo R. Browne, ed. (New York, 1961), p. 104.

Bibliography

ALBION, ROBERT G., *The Rise of the Port of New York, 1815–1860.* New York, 1970.

BARNUM, PHINEAS T., *Barnum's Own Story: The Autobiography*, Waldo R. Browne, ed. New York, 1961.

BILLINGTON, RAY A., *Westward Expansion.* New York, 1949.

BOATRIGHT, MODY C., *Folk Laughter on the American Frontier.* New York, 1949.

BODE, CARL, *The American Lyceum.* New York, 1956.

——, *The Anatomy of American Popular Culture, 1840–1861.* New York, 1959.

BUCK, SOLON, and BUCK, ELIZABETH H., *The Planting of Civilization in Western Pennsylvania.* Pittsburgh, 1939.

BULEY, ROSCOE C., *The Old Northwest, Pioneer Period, 1815–1840.* Indianapolis, 1950.

CARTWRIGHT, PETER, *Autobiography of Peter Cartwright, the Backwoods Preacher.* Cincinnati, 1856.

CHEVALIER, MICHAEL, *Society, Manners, and Politics in the United States: Letters on North America*, John W. Ward, ed. New York, 1961.

CLARK, A. H., *The Clipper Ship Era.* New York, 1910.

CLEMENS, SAMUEL ["Mark Twain"], *Life on the Mississippi.* Boston, 1883 and many later editions.

COLE, ARTHUR C., *The Irrepressible Conflict, 1850–1865*. A History of American Life series, vol. VII. New York, 1934.

COLLES, CHRISTOPHER, *Roads of the U.S.A*. Cambridge, Mass., 1961.

CURTI, MERLE, *The Growth of American Thought*. New York, 1943.

CUTLER, C. C., *Greyhounds of the Sea: The Story of the American Clipper Ship*. New York, 1930.

DANIELS, JONATHAN, *The Devil's Backbone: The Story of the Natchez Trace*. New York, 1962.

DAVIS, DAVID B., *The Problem of Slavery in Western Culture*. Ithaca, N.Y., 1966.

DRAKE, DANIEL, *Pioneer Life in Kentucky, 1785–1800*. New York, 1948.

DUNAWAY, W. F., *The Scotch-Irish of Colonial Pennsylvania*. Chapel Hill, N.C., 1944.

EVERY, DALE VAN, *Men of the Western Waters*. Boston, 1956.

FAULKNER, HAROLD U., *American Economic History*. New York, 1924.

FAUST, A. B., *The German Element in the United States*. 2 vols., Boston, 1909.

FISH, CARL R., *The Rise of the Common Man, 1830–1850*. A History of American Life series, vol. VI. New York, 1927.

FOSTER, SIR AUGUSTUS JOHN, *Jeffersonian America*, Richard B. Davis, ed. San Marino, Calif., 1954.

GREGG, JOSIAH, *Commerce of the Prairies*. New York, 1844; reissued Norman, Okla., 1954 and frequently elsewhere. 2 vols.

HANDLIN, OSCAR, *This Was America*. Cambridge, Mass., 1949.

HOLBROOK, STEWART H., *The Story of American Railroads*. New York, 1947.

HULBERT, ARCHER B., *The Historic Highways of America*. Cleveland, Ohio, 1905.

KROUT, JOHN A., and FOX, DIXON R., *The Completion of Independence, 1790–1830*. A History of American Life series, vol. V. New York, 1944.

MILLER, JOHN C., *The Federalist Era*. New York, 1960.

A Mirror for Americans: Life and Manners in the United States, 1790–1870, as Recorded by American Travelers, Warren S. Tryon, ed. Chicago, 1950. 3 vols.

MIRSKY, JEANNETTE, and NEVINS, ALLAN, *The World of Eli Whitney*. New York, 1952.

MORISON, SAMUEL E., and COMMAGER, HENRY S., *The Growth of the American Republic*. New York, 1942. 2 vols.

SCHLESINGER, ARTHUR M., SR., *Learning How to Behave*. New York, 1947.

SMITH, MARGARET BAYARD, *The First Forty Years of Washington Society*, Gaillard Hunt, ed. New York, 1906.

The South Carolina Rice Plantation as Revealed in the Papers of Robert F. W. Allston, J. H. Easterby, ed. Chicago, 1945.

STACKPOLE, EDOUARD, *Sea-Hunters: The New England Whalemen During Two Centuries*. Philadelphia, 1953.

STAMP, KENNETH M., *The Peculiar Institution: Slavery in the Ante-Bellum South*. New York, 1956.

SWEET, WILLIAM W., *Religion in the Development of American Culture, 1765–1840*. New York, 1952.

TROLLOPE, FRANCES, *Domestic Manners of the Americans*, Donald Smalley, ed. New York, 1949.

WEST, RAY B., *Kingdom of the Saints: The Story of Brigham Young and the Mormons*. New York, 1957.

WHIPPLE, A. B. C., *Yankee Whalers in the South Seas*. New York, 1954.

WRIGHT, LOUIS B., *Culture on the Moving Frontier*. Bloomington, Ind., 1955; reissued New York, 1961.

———, *Everyday Life on the American Frontier*. New York, 1968.

———, *Everyday Life in Colonial America*. New York, 1965.

WRIGHT, LOUIS B., and FRY, MARY ISABEL, *Puritans in the South Seas*. New York, 1936.

WYLLIE, IRVIN G., *The Self-Made Man in America*. New Brunswick, N.J., 1954.

YOUNG, JAMES H., *The Toadstool Millionaires: A Social History of Patent Medicines in America Before Federal Regulation*. Princeton, N.J., 1961.

Index

252

253

254

The Authors

Louis B. Wright, a noted American scholar, was director of the Folger Shakespeare Library in Washington, D.C., from 1948 until his retirement from that post in 1968. Since then he has been active as a consultant for the National Geographic Society and other organizations. He has published numerous works in the fields of American civilization and the English Renaissance. Holding a doctorate degree from the University of North Carolina, he has been the recipient of many honorary degrees from leading American and English universities. In 1968 Queen Elizabeth II appointed him Honorary Officer of the British Empire for his distinction in Anglo-American history. His most recent popular book from Putnam's was *Everyday Life on the American Frontier*. His home is in Chevy Chase, Maryland.

Elaine W. Fowler was for many years engaged in library and editorial work at the Folger Shakespeare Library. A specialist in the history of exploration and discovery, she is co-author with Louis B. Wright of *West and By North: North America Seen Through the Eyes of Its Seafaring Discoverers* (1971) and *The Moving Frontier: North America Seen Through the Eyes of Its Pioneer Discoverers* (1972). She is also author of *English Sea Power in the Early Tudor Period, 1485–1558* (1965). A graduate of Wellesley College, she now makes her home in Alexandria, Virginia. Her husband is a retired captain in the U.S. Navy.

256